TOUGHEST OF THEM ALL

is a collection of stories based upon an exhaustive study of court records, newspapers, books, and personal interviews with men and women closely connected with the people and events described. These are the only sources available; yet the material they furnish is necessarily incomplete, subject to the distortion, exaggeration, and bias of the times and of the tellers. The best any writer can do is to sift from that material what seems to him to be the truth. This Mr. Shirley has done. As to whether he has succeeded or not there will be differing opinions. But there will be few, we think, who will put this book aside unfinished—few who will finish it without having obtained a broader picture of the Old West and its people.

TOUGHEST OF THEM ALL

KATE BENDER · HENDRY BROWN · BOB OLLINGER · THE MARLOWS · SILON LE

Toughest of Them All

FRANK EATON · NELSON STORY · OLIVER W. WHEELER

...PLE HOUSTON · ZIP WYATT · DOOLIN GANG · CHEROKEE BILL

by

GLENN SHIRLEY

Copyright 1953
UNIVERSITY OF NEW MEXICO PRESS
Albuquerque

PREFACE

Much has been written about many of the colorful actors on our Western frontier. There are a few about whom very little, and in some cases practically nothing, has been written or said.

In this saga of the Old West, I write of these favorite few who were a cross section of the development of western America—cattlemen, lawmen, renegades, lawyers, judges, and gun-slingers. Some were good, some were bad. All were tough in their own hard way.

Some were tough because they were iron-nerved and determined, some fear-proof and conscience-proof, some incorrigible. I have here attempted to preserve a brief picture of each one's private side show. Although they have been given little consideration, they were, perhaps, the toughest of them all.

GLENN SHIRLEY

Stillwater, Oklahoma

CONTENTS

CHAPTER I

Saga of Pistol Pete

FRANK EATON

No saga of the Old West is more amazing than the one of Pistol Pete—badmen's nemesis. His real name was Frank Eaton. At a tender age he earned his reputation and that title handling a pair of heavy, single-action six-shooters that soon were to leave a bloody trail across the Southwestern frontier.

*   *   *

The moon rode high and full in a cloudless sky on a summer night in 1868. It was so quiet one could hear the whisper of the breeze across the Kansas prairie. At their home eight miles west of Carbondale, in Osage County, the Eaton family was preparing to retire.

The silence outside was shattered by the drum of hoofs. The horsemen swung into the yard and threw gravel clattering against the side of the house as they halted near the front porch.

"Eaton!" a heavy voice called out. "Frank Eaton!"

Inside the house the elder Eaton rose to his feet. His wife cautioned him not to go out. But Eaton, his face expressionless, told her calmly:

"Something has happened—probably Mose Beaman and the boys coming for help."

Mose Beaman commanded the Vigilantes—a group of Northern men who had banded together to protect the citizens against a lawless gang of Southerners called the Regulators, who rode at night, often in disguise, and pillaged and destroyed and stole stock from emigrant trains going west along the Santa Fe Trail. Frank Eaton was a Civil War veteran from Connecticut, who had joined the rush to Kansas in 1868. William Clarke Quantrill and his guerrillas had burned an old inn along the trail in their retreat from Lawrence, in 1863.[1] On this site, near the farm of Mose Beaman, Eaton had built his home.[2] He soon became embroiled in the fighting between the two factions.

"Maybe they have located the Campseys," he added as he stepped to the door.

The Campseys were a bad bunch. They lived a short distance from the Eatons, across Rock Springs draw. They rode with the Regulators and had ridden with Quantrill's raiders during the war. Their place was a hideout for ques-

1. J. P. Burch, *Charles W. Quantrill, a True History of His Guerrilla Warfare on the Missouri and Kansas Border During the Civil War of 1861 to 1865,* pp. 151–2.

2. Frank Eaton, *Pistol Pete, Veteran of the Old West,* p. 5.

tionable characters. The farm was owned by Shannon Campsey and his three brothers, Jim, Jonce, and Wyley. The Ferber brothers, Doc and John, spent a lot of time there. Only that day, Eaton had been responsible for a tip that had led to the location of several stolen horses on the Campsey place, and the sheriff and his posse had been searching for the brothers and the two Ferbers, who had fled.

Eaton opened the door and paused with the lamplight at his back. Too late he realized his mistake. A half dozen six-shooters covered him.

"Outside, you damn Yankee!" one of the riders shouted. "Come out and get what's coming to you."

Eaton, hands raised high, stepped to the edge of the porch. Tall and slender, clad only in nightclothes, he was standing like that when little eight-year-old Frank crowded to the door. He saw the blast of gunfire that knocked his father off his feet, saw him crumple on the hard, dry earth of the yard and heard his mother scream in terror. The killers spurred forward, shooing the child inside with their revolvers. Then they fired a second volley into the body and raked the front door with a fusillade.[3]

"Remember that, you God-damn Yankees!" the leader shouted back as they turned their horses and rode away into the night.

Little Frank remembered. He had seen their faces in the moonlight and never forgot them. The four Campseys and the two Ferbers. Lying across the body of his father,

3. "Life of Frank Eaton," *Guthrie Daily Leader,* April 16, 1939.

sobbing, while his mother fled to the home of their nearest neighbor for help, the child swore a grim oath.

Mose Beaman gave him his first pistol—an old Navy revolver with an eight-inch barrel. For two years he practiced drawing and firing, right hand, left hand. By the time he reached his tenth birthday, his draw was quick and smooth and his small thumbs flicked the hammer with amazing rapidity.

In the fall of 1869 his mother married again, sold the farm, and moved to southern Kansas, on Onion Creek west of Coffeyville, moving again a year later to the Cherokee Nation in Indian Territory.

Soldiers were considered the best marksmen in the country at the time. Young Frank spent his days around Fort Gibson, where the Sixth Cavalry was stationed under the command of Colonel Copinger.

The soldiers liked the boy. They fed him, raced horses with him, and shot against him. They were experts with their carbines. With their Army revolvers they could knock a crow off a pine stump at fifty yards. But little Frank, with his heavy pistol thonged to his slender leg, drew and outshot the best of them. Colonel Copinger was so impressed that he awarded the lad a gold medal and nicknamed him "Pistol Pete." [4]

Frank not only matched shots with the soldiers. Big Jim Starr, of the Cherokees, heard about him and invited him to pistol matches held by his tribe. Little Frank competed

4. "Pistol Pete, A Biography of Frank Eaton," *Tulsa World*, May 19, 1935.

with the best marksmen at the council meetings, and was proclaimed the best shot in Cooweescoowee District. Big Jim Starr gave him a Colt forty-five and his first two boxes of factory-made ammunition.

In 1875, when Frank was fifteen, he began riding the range for Osage Brown, a cattleman on Mission Creek in the Osage Nation. The cattlemen were having lots of trouble with horse thieves and rustlers, and one day while talking to some Cherokee cowboys from a nearby range, Frank learned that much of the stolen stock was being disposed of through two men, named Shannon Campsey and Doc Ferber, who were living on the Canadian River, southwest of Webbers Falls. It was the first word he had received about any of his father's murderers, and Frank rode south eagerly, following directions given him by the Indians.

The cabin was located in a clearing at the head of a draw, near a little creek. A high picket fence surrounded it and a log porch ran across the front. Shannon Campsey sat on the porch, watching the draw. As Frank approached, he saw Campsey get up and go inside. He reappeared a moment later with a Winchester. He sat down in his chair with the rifle across his lap and waited.

Frank rode up to the fence and dismounted. As he opened the picket gate, Campsey rose to his feet.

"Stop where you are, youngster!" he ordered. "Who are you, and what do you want?"

Frank was already through the gate. Nothing interfered in the dozen yards that separated them.

"I didn't figure you would recognize me, Shan," the boy replied. "I was just a little tike the night you shot down my father."

Campsey jerked his rifle to level in a split second. But that was too long. He died, doubled in a heap on the edge of the porch steps, with his face on the ground and crimson trickling out across the stock of the Winchester which he had never fired.

Frank leaped back on his horse, gun still in hand, looking sharply about for Doc Ferber. When no one appeared, he rode around the house. There was a trail where several cattle had been driven up the ravine toward a patch of timber, and Frank followed it cautiously. He had ridden only a few hundred yards when the wind brought him a whiff of burned hair and hide, and he knew someone was in the woods branding cattle. He reached the head of the ravine and started across a little clearing, angling toward the woods, when suddenly a rider burst from the trees and rode toward him.

"Hello, boy," he called, "what are you doing here? I thought I heard a shot."

"You did," Frank replied. "That was Shan Campsey. I came up here looking for a couple of fellows. Shan tried to stop me."

"What the hell—" stammered Doc Ferber. "Who are you? Who you want?"

"I want you, Doc, don't you know? You're one of the men who killed my father. Draw your gun, you son of a bitch!"

TOUGHEST OF
THEM ALL

Doc was already reaching for his six-shooter. But he was too slow. He fell forward off his horse, and Frank left him dead on the prairie with two bullet holes in his breast.

The cattlemen were not bothered with rustlers again for a while. Frank was lauded for his lone-hand play against two cattle thieves and was appointed detective for the Cattlemen's Association.

Shannon Campsey and Doc Ferber had been rebranding the stolen cattle for resale in Missouri. Checking this out, Frank learned that their Missouri contact was John Ferber, another of his father's killers, now living at Southwest City. Frank rode north; but, the night before he arrived, Ferber was shot for stealing a jack from the bottom of the deck in a poker game. Frank stayed for the funeral and inquired around Southwest City. He learned that Jim and Jonce Campsey had a little ranch up in the Ozarks.

The next morning he rode up in the hills. He rode all day before he reached their cabin, which stood at the edge of a spring in a clearing. It was almost supper time and Jonce Campsey was at a bench outside the door washing his hands. His brother wasn't in sight, and Frank wondered where he might be.

So he asked: "Is this where Jim and Jonce Campsey live?"

The man nodded.

"Are you Jim?" asked Frank. He was still trying to locate Jim.

"I'm Jonce," was the short reply.

So Frank said, "I have a message for Jim from John

Ferber, who was shot at Southwest City. I can't give it to anyone but Jim."

This remark brought Jim Campsey from the house with a rifle in his hand.

"I'm Jim," he said. "What did John say to tell me?"

Frank dismounted and deliberately walked closer to the two men, taking his time. When he was within a few feet of them, he said: "I'm Frank Eaton, and I'm going to kill both of you!"

Jonce reached for his six-shooter and Jim swung his rifle around. Jim died like Shannon Campsey, on the porch of his home with his Winchester under him. Jonce got his revolver clear of its holster, but the only shot he fired was in the ground as he fell. On their ranch Frank found numerous horses and cattle bearing the brands of over half a dozen outfits in the Cherokee Nation.[5]

The ranchers came to Missouri and rounded up their stock, and Frank rode back with them to Indian Territory. Five of his father's murderers were dead. He carved five notches on the handle of the forty-five Colt given him by Big Jim Starr, the Cherokee. Only Wyley Campsey clung to the end of his list. But the trail was cold now, and Frank continued on for a while punching cattle and as detective for the association.

His father's brother, Nick Eaton, began having trouble with Mexican cattle thieves in west Texas, and Frank rode out in the Panhandle to give him a hand. Uncle Nick had his ranch up on Running Water Creek, near the large

5. Frank Eaton, *Veteran of the Old West*, pp. 78–9.

ranges of Colonel Charles Goodnight and Deaf Smith. He was on the executive committee of the Panhandle Cattlemen's Association,[6] and through him, Frank was introduced to Colonel Goodnight. It was roundup time, and the Colonel gave him a job gathering cattle for the famous J A. It is a source of pride to Eaton today that he and Goodnight's nephew, Rolla Goodnight, later roped the first buffalo calves which formed the foundation for the famous Goodnight buffalo herd.[7]

While a cowboy for Goodnight, Frank made two trips up the Chisholm Trail, driving longhorns from Abilene, Texas, to the Sioux Pine Ridge agency in South Dakota. Afterwards he was employed to hunt stolen stock for the cattlemen's associations in New Mexico and Arizona.[8]

With the Apache outbreak, in the summer of 1885, Frank joined Captain Emmett Crawford's Warm Springs band to fight the crafty Geronimo and his renegade forces, and served as scout alongside Tom Horn, Al Sieber, Arizona Bill Gardner, and others. It was during the Apache warfare that he was almost scalped, but was saved by the timely arrival of his comrades.[9]

Frank returned to Indian Territory and soon was com-

6. J. Evetts Haley, *Charles Goodnight, Cowman and Plainsman,* p. 365.

7. In 1878, Colonel Goodnight, appalled at the wholesale slaughter of buffalo by the hide hunters of the seventies, had all the calves he could find in the Texas Panhandle rounded up and put under fence in order to perpetuate the breed. These calves developed into a herd of more than two hundred buffalo.

8. "Pistol Pete, a Biography of Frank Eaton," *Tulsa World,* May 19, 1935.

9. "I was unconscious from a bullet wound and the Indians had started to work with their scalping knives," says Eaton today, as he bows his head to show the scars. "But they hadn't quite finished the job before the soldiers came. The soldiers patched me up and I lived to fight some more."

missioned a deputy United States marshal out of Judge Isaac Charles Parker's "hanging" court, at Fort Smith, Arkansas. The court at that time had jurisdiction over approximately 74,000 square miles and 70,000 people.[10] Outlaws from every state and territory had found the Indian country an ideal place for hiding, and showed little respect for the two hundred marshals Parker sent into the area to ferret them out; sixty-five of these officers were killed in the line of duty.[11]

Frank's work now served a double purpose—it was a job for which he had developed an inclination—man hunting, and it kept his gun hands in perfect tune for the showdown with Wyley Campsey, if and when the day ever came. He added five more notches to his "old reliable" forty-five, and played a part in bringing many of the territory's worst desperadoes in on the hoof. Finally he learned that the sixth of his father's killers was tending bar in Albuquerque, New Mexico.

Again Frank Eaton rode west. Nothing about him had changed during all these years. It was a job he had to do. He had sworn an oath over the dead body of his father, and he would never rest until the last of the slayers had been accounted for.

One night several weeks later he rode into Albuquerque. While he was canvassing the saloons, a long-legged, somber-faced man stepped behind him into a patch of lamplight. Frank turned and strode back.

10. S. W. Harmon, *Hell on the Border; He Hanged Eighty-eight Men,* pp. 48–51.
11. *Ibid.*

II

"Stranger, are you following me?" he asked. "My name's Frank Eaton—from Indian Territory."

The other said grimly, "My name is Pat Garrett."

Frank looked at him with new interest. The whole West was still talking about Pat Garrett, who had shot Billy the Kid and ended the Lincoln County War.

"It's a privilege to meet you," Frank said. "Are you the sheriff here?"

Garrett said he was not. "I have been watching you go in and out of the saloons and you don't even smell of whiskey. If you're looking for somebody, maybe I can be of help."

Frank bluntly told him he was and gave the reason. "I have him located. He's tending bar in that place I just come out of. His name's Wyley Campsey."

Garrett looked worried. "Campsey's a bad hombre, son. He's been in a lot of trouble, and his two bodyguards are a couple of gunmen from Lincoln County—as dangerous as any men in New Mexico."

Frank laughed at Garrett's concern. "The odds aren't high enough," he said carelessly.

The famous sheriff studied him a minute, observing the notches cut in his six-shooter. "When you go up against two men and come out with a whole skin, you're lucky," he said finally. "But three to one is a hard game, son. I'll be waiting to see how you come out." He walked on up the street.

Frank opened the doors and paused inside. Campsey was at the end of the bar, talking with his two hirelings. Thus together, Frank could watch all three of them. He couldn't have asked for a better arrangement if he had planned it. He slapped his holsters with his hands, gave his body a quick twist inside his belt to settle his guns in position, and walked straight through the crowd toward the trio.

A few paces from them he stopped. He saw the stocky bartender stiffen. The two gunmen stepped back from him slightly. Quietly, Frank informed Wyley Campsey of his identity, then said:

"Go for your gun!"

For an instant the bartender was stunned. Then his hand darted to the ledge beneath the counter. Before he could lift his revolver above the bar, Campsey died with two bullets through his heart. The guards had drawn their weapons. One of them shot Frank in the hip and sat him down. A bullet from the other gunman's six-shooter tore into his left arm above the wrist, knocking the gun from his left hand. When the shooting started, the crowd had stampeded. In the confusion, someone shot out the light, and Frank crawled outside into the arms of Pat Garrett.

Garrett glanced at the wounds in his hip and his arm, then said: "Well, you came out all right, but you lost one of your guns. Here, take mine, and get out of town before they kill you."

Garrett took a revolver from his belt and slid it into Frank's empty holster. "A few miles out," he said, "you will see a 'dobie sprawling off to your right. Go there; tell the people I sent you. You will be among friends until you are able to ride on."

TOUGHEST OF
THEM ALL

Frank thanked him and galloped out of town.

The next day, Frank was well on his way back to Indian Territory. He hunted up a doctor friend, and soon recovered from his wounds. He went back to his old job as deputy marshal and spent another year chasing horse thieves and whiskey peddlers for Judge Parker.

But his vengeance trail had ended, and Frank "got the urge" to settle down. In the fall of 1889, after Oklahoma had been opened to settlement, he purchased a homestead in Perkins and opened a small blacksmith shop.

He is a picturesque person today as he putters around the forge and anvil. He wears his hair long, braiding it during the weekdays and, on Sundays, brushing it out to stream down over his shoulders. His long hair means a lot to him. The Indians used to credit white men with long hair with special courage, for they deliberately flaunted their long locks in defiance of Indian scalping knives. Eaton doesn't say he's a brave man, and admits that he could have his hair cut now that scalping has gone out of style without any discredit to his courage.

"But I'm an old dog and ain't aiming to learn new tricks," he says.

Every new moon he trims the ends. That, he explains, keeps hair from cracking.

Visitors and passers-by often stop and stare curiously at him and the articles he keeps lying around—old guns, bullet moulds, powder horns, saddles. They all have histories, and they all remind Frank of some stirring event of an earlier day, particularly the two long-barreled six-shooters dangling from a peg on the shop wall. One of them blasted the life from the last of his father's slayers. The other, a gift from Pat Garrett, is the gun, he says, that killed Billy the Kid.

Eaton claims that after going to the house of Garrett's friends, as the famous sheriff suggested, his wounds were dressed. He spent the night with these people, and while the man was re-dressing his wounds the next morning, Eaton examined the gun Pat Garrett had placed in his holster. It was a hair-triggered Colt .44 with an eight-inch barrel. Garrett's friend also looked at the gun and handed it back to Eaton, saying, "You're mighty lucky. That's the gun Pat used when he killed Billy the Kid!" [12]

On the other hand, the late Jesus Baca, once sheriff at Santa Fe, claimed to have owned the weapon. Pat Garrett's daughter, Miss Elizabeth Garrett, of Roswell, New Mexico, declared before her death that the Tom Powers estate of El Paso had the gun; that her father loaned it to Tom Powers, owner of the Coney Island Saloon in El Paso, in 1903, and that it was on exhibition there when her father died in 1904.[13]

Perhaps Jesus Baca or Miss Garrett were right; perhaps Eaton is right. His "old reliable" forty-five bears eleven notches and his skill with a six-shooter is still almost unbelievable for a man of ninety. Frank says it's true, and that he'll "back it up with both guns." I have no desire to argue the point.

12. Frank Eaton, *Veteran of the Old West*, pp. 180–1.
13. George W. Coe, *Frontier Fighter*, pp. 156–7.

CHAPTER II

Challenge to the Sioux

NELSON STORY

At the end of the Civil War, Texas men, undaunted and unsubdued, reluctantly returned home to find their ranges overrun with untended, unbranded cattle. During four years' absence, their stock had multiplied into vast herds of wild, long-horned creatures. The Civil War had served as a four-year blockade of cattle movements. A few herds had been marketed by secretly swimming the Mississippi River below Vicksburg and delivery to the Confederate armies, but Union gunboats soon put an end to that.[1] With no outlet, it is estimated that Texas alone had four million head of cattle worth less than four dollars each. The time had come when "a man's poverty was estimated by the number of cattle he possessed." A barter system was set up wherein "one good saddle horse was worth seventy-five head of cattle."

1. Walter Prescott Webb, *The Great Plains*, p. 212.

The South was starving, but it had no money to purchase beef. Attempts to sell cattle by shipping them on boats to cities like Mobile and New Orleans resulted only in financial loss and bitter disappointment.

But a thousand miles away in Yankee Land almost fabulous prices were being paid for livestock. Beef was scarce in the North.[2] More and more farmers who had been raising some cattle in Illinois and Indiana turned their land to crops. With the demand for beef cattle welling up to the east and supply running rampant on the broad ranges to the southwest, it seemed simple and inevitable that the "four dollar cow" and the "forty dollar market" would meet. Broad distances had to be traversed, and the only method of transportation was wholesale drives on foot. It was a challenge to the wild, reckless spirit of the Texans. In the spring of 1866, 260,000 longhorns were road branded and pointed toward the North Star.[3]

The season was wet. Swollen rivers, lightning, and stampedes took their toll. But the drovers saved most of their cattle and shoved them across Red River into the Indian nations. Eagerly they anticipated their arrival at Sedalia, Missouri, then the nearest railhead and end of the drive.

It wasn't until they crawled up Kiamichi Valley toward the corner of Kansas that they found themselves encircled by hard-faced delegations of Choctaw, Chickasaw, Creek,

2. Howard R. Driggs, *Westward America*, p. 227.
3. Walter Prescott Webb, *The Great Plains*, p. 217.

Cherokee, and Seminole Indians. These tribes demanded the right to cut the herds in search of their own cattle. They asked payment for the grass devoured and fields trampled by the transient longhorns, a toll of ten cents on each head passing over their lands, and threatened to back up their demands with firearms.[4]

The drovers had waged constant war with the red men of Texas, and would rather have swapped lead than dicker with them. But these Indians held their lands under government treaties, and the Texans recognized simple justice.

They turned their herds eastward, circling the Ozarks north of Fort Smith, and drove across the Missouri border. This venture ended in disaster.

Spanish fever[5] broke out, and Missouri cattle died by the hundreds. Missouri newspapers protested; the legislature passed laws prohibiting the Texans from entering from the south; and armed bands of enraged citizens in the border counties took summary action to turn back the herds and protect their own cattle.[6]

Men who had been released from both the Northern and Southern armies, and now found themselves in desperate straits, took advantage of the situation. "The fear of Spanish fever was made the pretext for committing the grossest outrages, just as the late Civil War was a convenient pre-

4. Paul I. Wellman, *The Trampling Herd*, pp. 84–5.

5. A fever caused by "ticks"—a blood-sucking insect carried by the Texas cattle. The longhorns, over a period of years, had developed a general immunity to the disease, but other animals were susceptible to the "tick fever" and died from it.

6. Howard R. Driggs, *Westward America*, p. 278.

text for lawless plundering, outraging, and murdering of civil, quiet citizens." [7]

Renegade bands, disguised as farmers, swept the border, spreading terror and exacting tolls as high as two and three dollars a head. The Texans were raided, and their cattle stampeded and run northward. Some who tried to force their way through were lynched and murdered. "Could the prairies of Southeast Kansas and Southwest Missouri talk, they could tell many a thrilling, blood-curdling story of carnage, wrong, outrage, robbery and revenge, not excelled in the history of any banditta, or the annals of the most bloody savages." [8]

A few Texans financially able to pay tolls for their cattle and otherwise negotiate with the leaders of the mobs, were permitted to pass through to Sedalia and given safe conduct through the country to the railroad. The rest found themselves in a hopeless situation. The cattle stacked behind them at Baxter Springs. Winter came. The frost killed the grass and entire herds starved. Some tried to circle their cattle back through the Indian country, but prairie fires had been set and the grass destroyed behind them. Others sold out for any price offered. Later, they learned they had been paid with bogus checks and drafts, and finally returned to Texas, broke and ruined.

Among the cattlemen held up at Baxter Springs was a young man named Nelson Story. His anger mounted as he faced the alternative of being beaten by border ruffians,

7. Joseph G. McCoy, *Historic Sketches of the Cattle Trade of the West and Southwest*, p. 23.

8. *Ibid.*, pp. 21–2.

defrauded by glib-tongued strangers, or letting his herd starve on its feet. To purchase the privilege of exercising his inalienable right to take his stock unmolested to any market he might choose was immoral, he believed. Neither defeat nor loss of money on this venture fit Story's confident boldness and deliberate daring.

Nelson Story was born on a farm in Meigs County, Ohio, in 1838. Orphaned at fourteen, he had worked his way through two years in Ohio University, at Athens, and taught country school. Then he caught the Western fever. He rode a steamboat down the Ohio River, took another up the Missouri and landed in Kansas with less than forty dollars in his jeans. He had obtained a job with an outfit freighting west from Leavenworth, and within two years was operating his own wagon and oxen.

He soon bought another outfit. The discovery of gold in the vicinity of Pike's Peak, by two parties of miners, in 1858, brought a large migration to the mouth of Cherry Creek, where the towns of Denver and Auraria were founded. On May 6, the following year, John H. Gregory, an old Georgia miner, struck rich deposits in the mountains at the headwaters of Clear Creek,[9] and more towns sprang into being. The emigrants swarmed to Colorado, up the Platte, the Arkansas, and Smoky Hill River,[10] prepared to dig for gold, but without the foresight to provide food, or money for picks and shovels.[11] Merchants in towns along the Missouri laid in stocks of food and equipment; men of

9. Albert D. Richardson, *Beyond the Mississippi, 1857–1867*, p. 178.
10. *Ibid.*, pp. 175–7.
11. Dorothy Gardiner, *West of the River*, pp. 246–7.

the Rockies offered fabulous prices for the goods. Twenty-year-old Nelson Story moved his freighting business to Denver.

In 1852, gold had been discovered on the Hellgate, in Montana. Other strikes occurred with startling frequency in Idaho and Nevada, and hordes of miners poured westward over the Oregon and Bozeman trails. In Idaho alone, Governor Caleb Lyon estimated a population of fifty thousand people. Discovery of gold on Grasshopper Creek, in southwestern Montana, in 1862, brought three thousand prospectors rushing to the "diggings," and Bannack mushroomed overnight into the first territorial capital. The honor was seized the next year by Virginia City, fifty miles west, with the rush of ten thousand people to the great strike at Alder Gulch, between the Beaver Head and Madison rivers.[12] The excitement was too great for Story. He left Denver, went to Alder Gulch, built a store, and began freighting goods through Idaho.

With this mad rush came also the refuse of humanity. Henry Plummer finagled the job as sheriff; and organized the greatest band of road agents the West ever produced. Stagecoaches and gold shipments were robbed, and men killed, until the law-abiding people organized a citizens court and arrested and tried George Ives, one of Plummer's men, for murder.[13] Nelson Story helped jerk the dry-goods box from under Ives when they hanged him on the town's main street.[14] The part he played in the

12. Frederick Logan Paxson, *The Last American Frontier*, pp. 168–9.
13. Nathaniel Pitt Langford, *Vigilante Days and Ways*, pp. 288–304.
14. Hoffman Birney, *Vigilantes*, p. 209.

capture and execution of Ives earned for him the captaincy of one of the grim bodies of vigilantes who, in the next thirty-five days, cleaned out the lawless element by stretching the necks of Henry Plummer himself and twenty-two of his mob of hellions. He became a leading citizen of Alder Gulch.

But Story tired of being a merchant. He turned to mining, struck a rich placer deposit near Summit, and took out more than forty thousand dollars.

Shoveling gravel and washing out nuggets in a "rocker," however, was too monotonous. While still in Denver, Story had heard about the cheap cattle in Texas. The possibility of bringing a herd north for Eastern markets smacked of strong adventure and huge profits. He sold his claim, sewed ten thousand dollars inside his clothing, hired two young men, Bill Petty and Tom Allen, and set out for Texas.

In Fort Worth, [15] he purchased a thousand head of longhorns, hired a crew of Texas cowboys, and started north. He ducked toll collectors. Outlaws, both red and white, stampeded his cattle to collect money for regathering them. Grass fires were set to trap his herd; his equipment was pilfered and his mules stolen before he reached the Missouri border, where he found himself in the same plight as other cattlemen.

While others sold out and turned back, Story thought of the gold fields of Montana and Idaho and the beef-

15. Paul I. Wellman, *The Trampling Herd*, p. 96. Harold E. Briggs in *Frontiers of the Northwest* claims Dallas.

hungry miners who had gone there with no thought of producing food. Gold dust for beef! Even the poorest ox would bring a hundred dollars.[16] Blocked from eastern markets, faced with complete loss if he remained here, Story made a quick decision.

"We're going to Montana," he told his men. "You've had it tough so far. We've come five hundred miles, but before us lays two thousand more. None of you agreed to go that far. Any who want to pull out I'll pay off now."

"We'll stay," a tall, thin-faced youth said.

"I'm taking the Bozeman Trail," Story warned.

They knew what he meant. John Bozeman, of Georgia, had blazed the trail in the winter of 1862–63 by leading an emigrant party through the Powder River country, along the eastern base of the Big Horns to the Big Horn River and the Yellowstone to Virginia City. They had established a settlement in the valley of the Gallatin and called it Bozeman. This road was far shorter than any other to the gold fields. During 1864–65 the principal immigration into Montana was by the Bozeman road and across Bozeman Pass,[17] and the powerful Sioux nations had rebelled. No more whites in their country. One after another, emigrant parties had been butchered, and the Army had pronounced it "hostile and impossible." [18]

But the Texans agreed to go. There were no wages for them in Texas.

16. Merrill D. Beal, *The Story of Man in Yellowstone*, p. 161.
17. Peter Koch in Montana Historical Society *Collections*, Vol. II, p. 135.
18. Montana Historical Society *Collections*, Vol. II, p. 135.

Story shoved his herd out of the jam below Baxter Springs and headed west. He followed the Kansas border nearly two hundred miles, until he was beyond the last settlements, then turned north over Smoky Hill, driving up the Kaw River through Topeka, to Fort Leavenworth. If he could reach Montana, he would sell six hundred head and make a larger profit than if he had taken the whole herd east. With the few hundred left he would start a ranch in the Gallatin. And why not make still more money by taking through a train of supplies for the gold miners?

While the herd rested at Leavenworth, Story bought ox teams and wagons, loaded them with groceries and provisions, and hired experienced bullwhackers he had known from his own freighting days. There was lots of talk about Red Cloud, the Sioux chief. An unsuccessful campaign against the tribes, in 1865, had resulted in adoption of peaceful measures. A series of nine treaties had been signed with as many bands of Sioux, at Fort Sully, in October. During March, 1866, General Grenville M. Dodge had negotiated a temporary cessation of hostilities with the war bands within his department, and at Fort Laramie, peace terms were concluded with the sullen chiefs of the Ogallala and Brule.[19] Then, immediately, the government tried to break these treaties by demanding a right of way and protection for travelers through the Powder River country, demands which Red Cloud refused. Despite this refusal, the government had decided to open the Bozeman

19. LeRoy R. Hafen and Carl Coke Rister, *Western America,* p. 529.

Trail by erecting a chain of forts across Wyoming,[20] and Red Cloud was on the warpath.

Story listened to the talk. Philo Remington had just invented the breech-loading rifle. The breech, opening by a rotating block system, made reloading fast and easy. These rifles were almost unknown in the West.[21] Story had never seen anything except muzzle-loaders, but he had heard of the seven-shot Spencer carbines used in the Civil War. He purchased thirty of these new rifles and plenty of brass cartridges. His cowboys examined them with awe. He also armed all his men with Colt six-shooters.

A few days later the huge procession of wagons crawled out of Leavenworth along the Oregon Trail. Behind it followed the herd of Texas steers.

As the caravan moved up the Platte to Fort Laramie and turned along the Bozeman Trail, Army officers shook their heads.

"You're a damn fool, Story," they said. "The whole Powder River and Big Horn is swarming with Sioux. The only post on that trail is Fort Kearny, on the Piney. Already 150 people have been killed up there. You can't expect any help at Fort Reno—more red devils around it now than you have cattle—and with a handful of cowboys you haven't a chance."

Story listened to the warning. He realized the full signif-

20. One post, Fort Reno, had been completed. The building of Fort Kearny, beyond Fort Reno, was in process. Farther north, Fort C. F. Smith had been located, but not built.

21. Troops had the old style Springfields. The breech-loader type of rifle was not introduced on the plains for the forts until 1867.

icance of the events that soon were to culminate in the annihilation, by the Sioux, of Captain William J. Fetterman's command, near Fort Phil Kearny and, within a few more years, the Custer debacle of the Little Big Horn. But he boldly ignored them.

"I've got a cargo of Remington rapid-fire rifles," he replied. "I got twenty-seven fightin' boys, and every jack man of them had red scalps hanging from his belt before he left Texas. We're going to Montana!"

Before Story left Fort Laramie, two Civil War veterans, John C. Catlin and Steve Grover, arrived from Leavenworth on their way to Virginia City. They asked Story if they might join his train.

"If what the Army says is true, there's forty Sioux to the mile," said Story. "You'll have to fight."

"That's all we've done for three years," Catlin replied.

Story had twenty-nine men now, as they moved on, a thousand head of longhorns, and a train of oxen and wagons. The first day out they began to see the remains of freight and emigrant outfits that had preceded them. Wagons burned, bodies horribly mutilated. They saw war parties on the ridges and knew they were being watched constantly. Tension grew as they continued northward. But they were not attacked until they were within a half day's drive of Fort Reno.[22] A band of Sioux stormed over a ridge, left two of Story's cowboys pinned to the ground with arrows, and retreated to reform for a second charge.

22. Grace R. Hebard and Earl Brininstool, *The Bozeman Trail,* Vol. I, p. 230.

Story and his men opened up on them as the Indians poured in. It was the first real test for the Remingtons, and the redskins quickly retreated, dumfounded at the rapidity of the white man's fire. They didn't stay for another test; but they cut out a bunch of cattle and drove them into the badlands.

When John Catlin was relating the story, years later, he was asked: "How many cattle did you lose?"

"Not a single head. We followed them Indians into their camp and spread out on two sides. At Story's signal, we opened on them with those Remingtons. When we brought the cattle back, there were no Indians to object."

Story left his wounded men at Fort Reno and went on. Again Army officers warned him he would never get through. It was sixty-seven miles to Fort Phil Kearny, and Indians were seen all the way. But they didn't attack. Perhaps word of the fast shooting rifles already had passed among the tribes.

But soldiers stopped Story outside the half-completed fort. Jittery Colonel Henry B. Carrington ordered him to go no further into the Indian infested region with his herd. The grass near the post was needed for government stock and Story's outfit was forced to camp too far away to expect any aid from the fort.[23] Smarting under this military restraint, they built two corrals to hold the cattle.

Every night for the next few days, Story and his men were forced to beat off sneak attacks on his guards. One by one, he realized, these men would be picked off, until his

23. *Ibid.*, pp. 230–1.

TOUGHEST OF
THEM ALL

force was reduced to such a number that they could offer little resistance to a large attack.

The situation could end only in complete annihilation. Story appealed to the fickle Carrington, but the Colonel still refused to let him move. Story called his men together.

"Shall we stay here and die without a fight?" he asked. "Or shall we give the soldiers the slip and drive on?"

They took a vote, and all but one, George Dow, was in favor of taking the risk against the Sioux. Dow was promptly placed under arrest so he could not reveal the plan to the soldiers. In the dead of night, herd and wagon train moved out past the soldier guards. Daylight found the caravan far beyond the fort in the heart of Sioux country and Dow was released.

It was the most desperate venture in all Western history. The only sure safety was Fort Phil Kearny. Ahead the trail wound hundreds of miles through a dreary region of buttes and hills and rolling, treeless plains, and the Sioux were sixteen thousand strong. But that night of October 22, 1866, Nelson Story and his remaining twenty-seven men challenged the whole Sioux Nation.

Story now shifted his driving methods. He rode ahead and his riders protected the flanks and rear. In daylight he camped his outfit and grazed his beef and oxen under heavy guard. In the darkness he pushed onward. Twice great bands of savages swooped down on them, but their bows and arrows proved no match for the rapid-fire Remingtons. Story and his men whittled them down by the hundreds. Not only could the rifles be reloaded quickly, but they had far greater range than any weapon the Sioux had known. When the Indians regrouped at what they considered a safe distance following a charge, Story and his men would keep firing into them and more Indians and horses died. The Sioux were unwilling to accept such losses, and they realized they could never approach Story's outfit close enough to do effective work with their bows and arrows.

"There were three hundred troops at Fort Phil Kearny," Catlin recalled. "But the Indians were worse scared of us with our Remingtons than they were of the soldiers with their Springfields. After we got 'em scared, it was easy for twenty-seven of us to stand off three thousand reds." [24]

The night marches took the train to the site of Fort C. F. Smith and the villages of the Crows. From there they cut northwest across the Yellowstone and down Emigrant Gulch to Bozeman. On December 9, 1866, Story rolled his supply caravan and beef herd into Virginia City.

He sold six hundred cattle, started a ranch in the Gallatin, and built a store in Bozeman. When horse ranching began in western Montana, in 1876, he bought two hundred California mares and soon had a herd of thirteen hundred horses. He sold hundreds of young horses each year at fifty, seventy-five, and a hundred dollars a head.[25] He became the largest and wealthiest stock raiser in the state, built several more business houses in Bozeman, started the First National Bank, of which he was president, and

24. *Ibid.*, p. 231.
25. James S. Brisbin, *The Beef Bonanza*, pp. 140–5.

built a big flour mill. As a leader in civic affairs, he erected a monument over the grave of John Bozeman, the founder, on the brow of the bluff overlooking the city, and gave nearly all the sixty-acre campus of the Montana State College of Agriculture and Mechanical Arts when it was organized at Bozeman, in 1893. In 1892, he sold thirteen thousand blooded cattle, the largest sale of stock in the state, and went to Los Angeles to spend the winter. Here he invested his cattle money in real estate, and erected the Story Building, the city's first skyscraper. He died in 1926, at the age of eighty-eight.

He left a name and a fortune, but, more than that, he is remembered for his remarkable journey through Powder River valley while redskins swarmed there. The rich profits he realized from his daring prompted others to follow the Bozeman Trail; but Red Cloud, maddened by such effrontery, waged such savage war that, for four years, no other cattleman attempted to venture into the Wyoming wilds.

But Story had proved it could be done. It took tough men like him to carve a place for others on the raw frontier —men like him and his twenty-seven Texans, who, with him, drove through hell.

CHALLENGE TO
THE SIOUX

CHAPTER III

Sacramento Colonel

OLIVER W. WHEELER

In the spring of 1867, Texas cattle-men waited at Red River with anxious eyes turned north-ward, seeking a route around the delegations of the Five Civilized Tribes and the mobs of Missouri.

During the turbulent trail wars of 1866, tales of the cattle blockade in Indian Territory and at the Missouri border had reached Joseph G. McCoy an enterprising young cattle dealer in Springfield, Illinois. McCoy, his imagination fired, conceived the idea of routing the big herds straight north to some point on the railroad then being constructed to link Kansas City with Denver. Certain conditions had to be met. The cattle depot must be on a railway and at a convenient point far west of all settlement so the drovers would not again be blocked in their northern course. McCoy chose, finally, the small, unprepossessing hamlet of Abilene. It offered even additional advantages: It was surrounded by a sweeping sea of grass for grazing and fattening stock at the end of the drives, and it was near Fort Riley, which offered protection from Indian attack as well as an additional potential market for beef.

On the spur of the railroad he erected a two-story hotel, known as the Drovers Cottage, for the accommodation of the Texas cattle traders, built an office and set up his scales, and constructed a corral sufficiently strong to hold three thousand longhorns. The project, begun in July, was completed within sixty days. Meanwhile, McCoy had sent riders south to contact the Lone Star herds and tell their owners about Abilene, "a good, safe place to drive to," where they would be met by reputable Northern and Eastern buyers instead of thieves, and could sell or ship their cattle unmolested.[1]

This was encouraging news to the Texans. All they had to do was drive north away from Indian Territory and across Kansas to Abilene. Men's hearts leaped hopefully, but gazing northward these hopes began to fade and die. They recalled the terror and outrage and robbery in their futile attempts to drive through Arkansas and Missouri. "The fear of trouble and violence hung like an incubus over their waking thoughts alike with sleeping moments. . . . They were very suspicious that some trap was set, to be sprung on them; they were not ready to credit the proposition that the day of fair dealing had dawned for Texan drovers, and the era of mobs, brutal murder, and arbitrary proscription ended forever." [2]

1. Joseph G. McCoy, *Historic Sketches of the Cattle Trade of the West and Southwest,* pp. 39–50.

2. *Ibid.,* p. 51.

Too, between them and Kansas lay hundreds of miles of wild, uncivilized country, traversed by marauding tribes of Plains Indians. What new violence awaited them in this unknown frontier? Behind, an ever-increasing number of cattle pressed close to the river. The season was waning; still they hesitated. Who would be first "to turn their herds toward the point designated" and break a trail through an uncharted wilderness.

Among the cattlemen was a small, insignificant looking little Californian named Oliver W. Wheeler. He was born in Connecticut in 1826. Members of his family were wealthy stockmen of that state. He had learned stock-raising on the farm, and attended institutions of higher learning to obtain the best training possible in his chosen field. Still a young man, well equipped for a successful business career, he had embarked to build his fortune in the East, when he was suddenly stricken with tuberculosis of the lungs.

Physicians gave him only months to live. Deciding not to die without a fight, the youth sought a change of climate in the gold digging of California.

This was two years after gold had been discovered at Sutter's mill, and the zest of life that permeated the gold fields imbued him with a spirit of bravery and fearlessness that soon brought him great success upon the Western plains.

Due to his slight stature and sapped strength, he was not able to perform labor in the mines. He obtained a position in the mercantile business at Sacramento. Here he purchased a large number of cattle and horses. These he took to the mountains and desert where he traded and sold them to emigrants who had worn out their own stock in their long trek across the plains. He not only made considerable money, but the very nature of the work improved his physical condition, though the malady left him an emaciated body the rest of his life.

With his new fortune, he began freighting to the mining camps. On the side, he dabbled in the sheep business and made enough money to go south to Los Angeles and purchase a large herd of cattle, which he drove north and disposed of at a huge profit. In southern California, he bought a big cattle ranch, which he sold within a year at another good profit, keeping a portion of the cattle. He drove this herd to San Francisco and opened a wholesale meat market, which consumed forty head daily. This soon exhausted his herd, but he obtained a supply from others, and continued to operate the wholesale meat business for two years.

After ten years, Wheeler went back to his native Connecticut, a well man. But the West had put its stamp on him. He decided to return to California and take a large herd of horses.

This was in 1861, and the Indians were on the warpath, roving wild, killing every human being and waylaying every caravan they could find. Crossing the plains was dangerous enough, and the Indians were especially fond of horses. But Wheeler's experiences in the West had taught him a lot about redskins. To prevent capture, robbery, and even massacre, it was necessary to travel in large numbers. For this new venture he amassed the greatest train of emigrants and plainsmen ever to cross the continent. Although no records have been preserved, it has been estimated that the caravan contained from six hundred to eight hundred persons.[3] These people unanimously elected Wheeler to command the undertaking and gave him the title of "Colonel"—a designation he carried the rest of his life.

With several hundred wagons and over a thousand head of loose stock, Colonel Wheeler moved west. It was a tedious journey through sere desert wastes and lands declared forbidden to the white-skinned invader. Bleached bones of luckless travelers bore mute testimony of the ruthless determination of the Plains Tribes to keep out the white man. Throughout the trip, war-painted savages lurked on hilltops and canyon rim, watching the vast string of covered wagons creeping past, waiting to catch the train unawares. They noted the manner in which it traveled and knew it was in charge of an experienced leader. They were given no chance to attack this immense, semi-military organization, and the entire caravan arrived in California without the loss of a single life because of Indians.[4]

Wheeler sold his horses. The proceeds he invested in fat cattle in Lower California, drove them to the mining camps in the northern part of the state and the great silver

3. Paul I. Wellman, *The Trampling Herd*, p. 134.
4. Joseph G. McCoy, *Historic Sketches of the Cattle Trade of the West and Southwest*, p. 260.

TOUGHEST OF
THEM ALL

regions of Nevada, and continued to prosper. Then the big drought of 1866, accompanied by a grave scarcity of cattle, swept the Pacific slope. The chief fount of Wheeler's great fortune was destroyed.

The little colonel didn't wait for the industry to build up again. Associating himself with a Mr. Hicks and a Mr. Wilson, he crossed the plains to Texas by way of El Paso and purchased 2,400 longhorns to drive back to California. His plan was to cross the Indian Territory to a point near Abilene, then proceed west along the Platte on the California trail through South Pass, the route he had followed with the emigrant train. But what new obstacles waited in that unknown strip between Texas and the Cimarron?

The bands of soldiers that had ventured into it in their campaign against the Plains Tribes had been led by experienced guides. To explore a route and drive a large herd of cattle across it at the same time seemed next to impossible.

While the others hesitated, the fearless little drover made preparations to meet this strange and challenging danger. He purchased over a hundred of the best cow horses he could find. He hired fifty-four of the best cowboys, who were also qualified Indian fighters, and armed each man with a Colt revolving six-shooter and a Henry repeating rifle, the last word in Indian-fighting weapons.

No more complete an outfit or a better herd of cattle ever left Texas.[5] "They were a formidable array. Conchos

5. *Ibid.*, p. 261.

glistened on the head stalls of their bridles, their long leather tapaderas trailed down from their stirrups, their large Spanish spurs dragged the ground and jingled a merry tune as they walked or rode. New stiff chaparajos adorned the legs of every rider. Their wiry mustangs jumped and snorted at every move of the rider. On the right side, looped by a string to the saddle horn, hung the ever present riata, made of good rawhide. From the left side, with the loop on the handle around the saddle horn, hung the cowboy's quirt, less than three feet long, but the only whip he ever used." [6]

Thus equipped, the huge outfit moved out from San Antonio in the early summer of 1867. It crossed the Colorado River near Austin, and the Red River into hell. Storms blasted in all their fury. Thunder and lightning, floods and stampedes took their toll. The heavy rains made the grass on the trail soft and washy, with little nutriment. The longhorns grew lean and worn.

But Wheeler, with his fighting crew, continued north, keeping his course in almost a direct line away from the raiding tribes to the west. He crossed the Canadian at a point fourteen miles east of the present city of El Reno, struck Kingfisher Creek and followed it to where it empties into the Cimarron. This point afterwards became the river crossing on the Chisholm Trail. [7]

After crossing the Cimarron, Wheeler took the Old Trader's Trail, laid out in 1865 by the half-breed Cherokee

6. Sam P. Ridings, *The Chisholm Trail*, p. 65.
7. *Ibid.*, p. 67.

freighter and guide, Jesse Chisholm. He traveled along it to the Indian Territory line, entering Kansas near Caldwell, and trailed his herd over the finest range he had ever seen. As the drive approached Abilene, reports came that the Asiatic cholera was sweeping the western plains. Up the Missouri and all along the overland trade routes, hundreds had died or were suffering from the malady. Added to these reports were new hostile outbreaks of the Indians. General W. S. Hancock had bungled the government's "peace policy" with his clumsy expedition against the Cheyennes, and they were devastating the frontiers. The Arapahoes had attacked several settlements in western Kansas, killing men, women, and children, and had torn up the tracks of the Union Pacific railroad in Nebraska. The Kiowas and Comanches were raiding in the Texas Panhandle and New Mexico. By the time Wheeler had driven his herd within thirty miles of Abilene, his partners had become so apprehensive they called a halt.

Wheeler was no "theorist or dreamer desiring to attempt impossibilities, but having often been exposed to savage redskins, and being anything but a coward, he did not fear to go forward with the herd and fight their way, if need be, through the hostile Indian country." [8] He cajoled and "earnestly urged" his two partners to carry out their original agreement, but they refused. Angry, too stubborn to sell, Wheeler held the herd on grass, and thus lost the honor of driving the first cattle to Abilene. The

8. Joseph G. McCoy, *Historic Sketches of the Cattle Trade of the West and Southwest,* p. 261.

SACRAMENTO
COLONEL

first herd to reach Abilene was driven by a man named Thompson, who had left Texas following Wheeler's trail, but in Indian Territory he had sold out to three speculators, named Smith, McCord, and Chandler, and it was driven by them past Wheeler's grazing herd to McCoy's corral.[9] After holding his cattle on grass for some time, Wheeler finally sold them in Abilene at a fair profit.

On September 5, the first shipment, consisting of twenty cars, left Abilene for Chicago. That night a big celebration was held as the stock buyers from the North and stock raisers from the South sat down to "feast, wine and song," heralding the beginning of the great cattle era that was to follow. It was too late to increase the drive from Texas that year. A few more scattered herds reached Abilene, and only 35,000 cattle were shipped in 1867. But news of the success of these drovers swept Texas, and McCoy put on a mammoth advertising campaign to bring more Northern buyers to Abilene to meet the Texas drovers, and in the next three years over 1,225,000 head of cattle were driven north over various trails to the Kansas cowtowns.[10]

Wheeler broke with Wilson and Hicks, and never again entered into partnership with anyone. But he realized that his future in the stock business lay in the central West. He went back to Texas. He bought five thousand more cattle and drove them to Nevada. He trailed another herd of six thousand to Abilene and sold these to the Chicago markets. In 1870, he drove over twelve thousand cattle

9. *Ibid.,* p. 51.
10. Edward Everett Dale, *Cow Country,* p. 32.

out of Texas. He drove seven thousand up the trail the following year, and, in 1872, he made a single sale of five thousand head for $125,000.[11] His judgment in these cattle ventures was uncanny. He saw the break coming in the business. After 1872, he did not drive or buy, avoiding the catastrophe in 1873.

As the railroad crawled westward, so did Wheeler's operations. In 1874, he went to Kansas City, where he suddenly disappeared. Where he went from there no one has ever learned. His resting place remains a mystery. But he was a man of daring spirit and keen judgment in the West's greatest industry.

His greatest achievement will ever be recorded as that drive across an unknown country, when he rode at the head of the first Texas longhorns ever to cross Indian Territory over the trail from Red River to the Cimarron.

11. Joseph G. McCoy, *Historic Sketches of the Cattle Trade of the West and Southwest*, p. 265.

SACRAMENTO
COLONEL

CHAPTER IV

Prairie Vampire

KATE BENDER

A chill wind whipped the prairie; overhead, dark brooding clouds scudded across the Kansas sky. A sliver of moon broke through, to light for a moment the grim, set faces of the eight men who stood in a semicircle on the banks of Verdigris Creek where it empties into Fall River, and revealed the scene of carnage about them.

As if the moon was their signal, seven of the men dropped to their knees. When all were down, the leader knelt also and raised his right hand. In slow, firm tones he recited a solemn oath of silence that each man repeated afterward, a violation of which meant death.

Thus, on the night of April 3, 1873, a cloak of secrecy was drawn over the mystery of the most diabolical orgies of the West—the atrocities of the Benders of Kansas.

*   *   *

Kate Bender was a young woman with auburn hair, curved, gracious, beautiful. Five feet six, 130 pounds, she held herself proudly erect, head high, alert hazel eyes wide and very bright. He lips were red—cherry red, and pouting. "It was a mouth to disturb the dreams of the young men who saw her," and the lonesome, weary stranger who came to the inn on the vast, trackless plains in the twilight of an evening in 1871 thought he was in luck. He had no idea what tragic horror lurked inside those four walls or that he had entered a nest of vicious killers.

While he ate, the young man's eyes followed the girl, who now moved quickly about the room, laughing and talking glibly, almost incessantly. The lamplight on the table cast his shadow against the curtain at his back. The watcher in the other room saw him only as a silhouette.

Old William Bender, Kate's father, was seated on a stool near the counter, reading the Bible. Though age had bowed his shoulders, he was a giant of a man, large boned, with a heavy jaw, high cheekbones, low forehead, and black, piercing eyes set under huge, bushy brows. Kate's mother was busy at the stove. She was about sixty years old, heavy with sickening white fat; dirty black hair streaked with gray. She watched the stranger through dark, heavy-lidded eyes, her expression savage and sullen.

Suddenly Kate stepped behind the counter. The young man shifted in his chair so his eyes could follow the girl. His head touched the curtain.

The watcher on the other side lifted the heavy hammer in his hand. It rose and fell with a thud. The man at the table slumped forward in his chair.

Then beautiful Kate Bender became a tigress. She leaped

from behind the counter. In her hand was a long knife.
The stranger struggled to sit up. He saw her red lips
twisted, her eyes gleaming, her full breasts rising and fall-
ing in savage delight as she sprang upon him and swung
the knife. The man dropped back and fell on the floor,
his head half severed.

Slowly old man Bender closed his Bible, laid it on the
stool and beckoned to his wife. Together they pushed
aside the stove and lifted a trap door. John Bender, Kate's
brother, came from behind the curtain with an aimless
little laugh. He was about twenty-five years old, tall,
florid, and rather good-looking "in an awkward, country-
boy style." But his eyes were "set too close together, shallow, and so wide opened as to give the effect of a stare."
He waited until Kate ran deft fingers through the stranger's clothing and removed all his money and valuables,
then helped the old man drag the limp form to the trap
door and dump it into a prepared pit below.

Kate Bender looked like a witch as she counted the
money and tucked it into her bodice. Then she straight-
ened her hair with her fingers, the evil spirit left her, and
she regained her smiling composure.

Kate Bender had slain her first victim.

The Benders had come to Kansas in the spring of this
year. Where they came from is a mystery. They never
told. One morning the community awoke to find the inn
going up on the prairie. The building was a one-roomed
frame affair with a wagon sheet and a patched quilt
hanging from the joists dividing off the rear room where

the Benders lived, ate and slept, and prepared meals for travelers. In the front room was the counter and some shelves on which tobacco, crackers, powder, shot, and provisions were displayed for sale. A few kegs and rough stools were provided to accommodate customers. It set on an isolated, thinly populated stretch of plain a dozen miles south of Thayer and a short hundred yards off the main road crossing Labette County, from Fort Scott and Old Osage Mission to Independence, over which hundreds of persons trekked into the sunset.[1] Above the doorway hung a sign bearing the single, poorly lettered word, GRO-CERIES. Behind the house to the north was a well and a stone barn. Just east of this was a combined garden and orchard with fifty fruit trees. It was carefully cultivated and thus furnished an excuse for constant harrowing and dig-ging.[2]

That night the first victim was dragged from the hole under the house and buried in the orchard. In the daylight the carefully worked ground gave no sign of the new grave.

A year passed, and one victim after another was lured from the trail by the inviting oasis and the beckoning lips of beautiful Kate Bender, only to forfeit their lives. In-variably they were men from faraway places, going west to settle and buy machinery, cattle, and horses; and they frequently carried large sums of money upon their persons.

1. The trail is slightly north of the route followed by U. S. 160. Visible from the highway are the Bender Mounds, low hills rising abruptly from a level plain. They were named for the Bender family. *Kansas, a Guide to the Sunflower State,* p. 425.

2. Edith Connelley Ross in *Collections of the Kansas State Historical Society, 1926–1928,* Vol. XVII, pp. 467–8.

In several instances, the missing persons were trailed to Thayer, and there all trace of them vanished. Mail in those days was uncertain. Inquiring relatives could only "take it for granted" that they had gone on into Indian Territory or Texas, or the great frontiers beyond. Even if their suspicions were aroused, how could they prove the fate of their loved ones?

"It was a situation so absolutely safe as to reassure and fortify even a coward. And whatever else they were, the Benders were certainly not nervous, fear-ridden people." While most criminals "flee from the ghost-ridden scene of their crime, and cower, sweating and shivering, at the very recollection of the spot," the Benders lived for a long time "undisturbed and with apparent placidity in the ghastly setting they had created, and surrounded by the decaying bodies of their victims." Whether they were so "stolid and unimaginative that murder was a matter-of-course to them" or "their number gave them confidence," robbery was a motive and it is obvious that they killed "for the morbid gratification and excitement, for the joy of the evil deed. . . ." [3]

None of the local people suspected the Benders. "This particular section of the country was settled by earnest, hard-working men and women, who were trying to wrest a living from the droughty, wind-swept plain. The constant struggle, the fierce contest with the land to obtain food and shelter, dulled their interest and curiosity concerning the world at large and even their own vicinity.

3. *Ibid.*, p. 468.

They accepted the newcomers at face value. Many people, most of whom time had proved to be good friends and honest, had come in this same manner and with as little to say of their former life. So why be curious concerning the affairs of one more emigrant family who were going to 'homestead'?" [4]

On the contrary, the Benders were considered respectable citizens. Old William Bender and his wife were "frankly hostile" to their neighbors and made known their desire to be left alone. Young John, however, was friendly enough. He was believed to be a half-wit, but there is evidence to show he was a very clever individual, and that his peculiar actions were only a disguise for his constant listening and watching. Kate was the sociable one. She liked company, and did everything to "cultivate" it. She went to church and sang and prayed. She laughed and talked and flirted with the young men of the community and was regarded by several "with distinct favor."

As added inducement for victims to visit her house of death, Kate also claimed a gift for second sight and spiritualism. She gave séances and claimed she could cure any disease, and had printed and distributed notices advertising her powers as follows:

Prof. Miss Katie Bender

Can heal all sorts of Diseases; can cure Blindness, Fits, Deafness and all such Diseases, also Deaf and Dumbness.

4. *Ibid.,* p. 465.

Residence, 14 miles east of Independence, the road from Independence to Osage Mission one and one-half miles South East of Morehead Station.

Katie Bender

June 18, 1872.

The Benders killed all their victims in the same manner —by crushing their skulls from behind with a hammer then slashing their throats. At variance, however, with the common belief that the deaths all occurred while the victims sat at the table with their backs to the curtain separating the two rooms while Kate, as waitress or medium, held their attention, is the incident related by their nearest neighbor, M. E. Sparks:

"One man told of his visit to the place, when, he believed, he had escaped death only because the Benders learned that he lived not far away. He had recently settled a few miles further west, and on the first occasion that his stock of provisions ran low he had concluded to go to the Bender store to see if he might replenish his larder there. Tying his horse before the house he entered and took a seat on a keg which occupied the center of the front room [while he] looked over the stock of goods [behind the counter] and talked to Mrs. Bender, who was waiting on him.

"Presently the old man emerged from behind the curtain which screened the back part of the place. Bender carried a hammer such as a blacksmith uses and as he came in he looked the customer over and inquired abruptly:

" 'Where did you come from?'

"He was apparently not satisfied with my friend's reply, for, a few minutes later, he asked again:

" 'Where did you say you live?' And for the third time Bender asked a similar question before my friend left the place. He was afterward confident that had he told Bender that he was a stranger in the country he would have received a blow from the hammer, of which he took little notice at the time, for he supposed it was carried for the purpose of opening a box.

"I believe they killed their victims anywhere and at any time they found an opportunity—always within the house, of course, but just as circumstances dictated. . . ."

Paradoxically, the Benders murdered only those from distant places so that safety was dependent upon living close to them.

They did not bury all their victims in the orchard, however. The body of at least one man—with his head smashed and throat cut—was found in Big Hill Creek, three miles from the Bender farm. He was never identified and it was thought the murder was committed by some transient criminal.

So, for two years, the Benders carried on their bloody orgies, robbing travelers of their cash and jewelry and disposing of their stock and equipment among the great mass of people moving west.

PRAIRIE
VAMPIRE

More and more searchers followed their loved ones to Thayer, then lost all trace of them. Strangers would be seen in Fort Scott or Independence, then vanish.

All this time the countryside was swept with rumors. Over store counters, at church, at school meetings, the situation was discussed and enlarged upon until people became afraid to ride to or from the towns at night. By the end of the second year a strange, uncomfortable feeling had settled over the community. Men looked at their neighbors with distrust and fear.

Talk began to circulate about the Benders.

On three different occasions, intended victims, suddenly seized with a feeling of danger, fled from the house with tales of shuddering terror.

One was an eccentric old woman named Hesler. She was the masculine type and traveled about the country alone with a shotgun. She was deeply interested in spiritualism, and visited Kate frequently. One evening, while she was at the Benders "communicating with ghosts," Kate began to perform in an amazing manner. Her eyes took on a glitter, her voice grew shrill, her body restless. Finally she leaped to her feet and drew a long-bladed knife. She drew pictures of men on the unpainted walls of the kitchen and stuck the knife into them. "The spirits often command me to kill, kill!" she cried. Suddenly she laughed wildly and whirled on the old woman. Her lips were drawn back, her nostrils flared and "her eyes seemed to flame green as a cat's in the twilight."

"They tell me to kill you—kill you—now!"

The frightened old woman fled. When she told her story afterwards, people refused to believe her. She was known to be queer and a trifle deranged, and they thought it only her imagination.

Another woman had gone to the Bender house to get a sidesaddle Kate had borrowed and not returned. She was seated at the table in the front room with her back against the curtain, talking, when suddenly Kate leaned forward, eyes glittering, nostrils flaring, and called in a loud, slow voice: "Now, now!"

When nothing happened, she leaned back in her chair and laughed and went on talking.

The woman thought nothing of it until, a few moments later, Kate again repeated the words in a louder voice.

Then John Bender's voice came from behind the curtain, agitated and broken: "No—no—by God, I can't do it. I can't! No—no."

The woman left shortly thereafter with her saddle, but terrified by the strange incident, and never went back to the Benders.

Father Paul Ponziglione, a priest traveling through the country, stopped at the Bender home one night for food and rest. He was not impressed by the family, and the atmosphere of tenseness and waiting made him apprehensive. Kate laughed and joked as she prepared to serve him, but he noticed how her eyes grew wide and bright and her face seemed to glow from some unholy joy within her. When he saw her father place a heavy hammer behind the curtain, he became afraid. He remembered the tales he had heard of how men had dropped off the earth in this very section. Suddenly Kate turned and started toward him. The priest leaped from his chair. Muttering something about having to see about his horse, he hurried from the house. Once outside, he leaped onto his mount and fled.

Doctor William H. York was the last man the Benders murdered. On March 10, he left sick relatives in Fort Scott to return to his home in Independence, and never arrived. His brother was Colonel A. M. York, a power in Kansas politics and later a member of the legislature. He was not a man "to let a relative disappear without making every effort to fathom the mystery," and when the worried family got in touch with the Colonel, he instituted a search at once.

York trailed his brother to Harvey Burns's farm a short distance northeast of Thayer. Here he learned that Doctor York had stopped to water his horse and inquire the distance to Osage Mission. Proceeding from Thayer to Osage Mission to make a further check there, he paused at the Bender place to ask if they had seen anything of his brother. The Benders denied they had, but Kate "spoke of her gift as a spiritualist medium and offered to place her talent at his disposal."

"I'll find your brother for you," she promised the Colonel, "even if he is in hell."

But Colonel York refused to séance. The brooding family and their malevolent looks told him something was wrong. As he started back to his horse he noticed an object gleaming in the dirt. He leaned over and picked up a flat, round-headed stickpin of the type worn seventy years ago. As he turned it over in his hand, his face paled.

It was the stickpin worn by his missing brother!

York mounted his horse quickly and rode away. Kate Bender, peering from the window, saw what had happened.

Two weeks later a neighbor stopped at the Benders and discovered the entire family missing. In the barn he found a calf dead from thirst. Other farm animals suffered from lack of attention. He went back to the house, found the door unlatched and stepped inside to investigate. He took one look and fled from the place in terror.

News was sent to Colonel York at once, who arrived with a searching party of citizens and entered the house of horror. They found the floor piled with old rags and several bloody weapons. The table was filled with dirty dishes. Everything else was in confusion, indicating a hasty departure.

They noticed the kitchen stove had been moved off the trap door and when the door was opened such a nauseating odor arose from the pit that no one would go down until the whole house had been placed on logs and rolled away.

There were no bodies in the pit, but the blood-stained rocks and soil revealed the use to which it had been put by the Benders.

By now the entire countryside was aroused. Searchers spread over every inch of the Bender farm. The preceding weeks had been dry, the patch of garden and orchard had not been worked and the earth had split in cracks as much as seven feet in length. Digging into these, they unearthed the body of Doctor York. His head had been crushed by a heavy blow, his throat slit, and part of his clothing was missing. Six other bodies, including that of a small child, were found in graves under a big apple tree. All except the child showed marks of vicious blows on the skulls and all their throats had been cut.

Meanwhile the Bender wagon had been discovered near Thayer,[5] a short distance from the railroad station. The local agent stated that he had sold tickets to two men and two women.

A hunt for the Benders spread throughout the nation. Hundreds of men and women thought to be the bloodthirsty quartet were held for investigation. Several were arrested on the charge. Mr. Sparks made trips to Denver, Colorado, and Fremont, Nebraska, and numerous other places to identify suspects, and Frank Deinst, sheriff of Labette County, traveled far and wide in his search for the slayers. In 1889, two women believed to be Kate Bender and her mother were arrested at Oswego, but cleared of suspicion and freed. Kate and her family had vanished as mysteriously as they had appeared on the Kansas prairie that night in '71.

As the years passed, reports on women alleged to be Kate Bender appeared in newspapers all over America and parts of Europe. Even as late as 1935 a story was flashed on the wire services throughout the country that Kate

5. *Thayer Headlight*, April 9, 1873.

TOUGHEST OF
THEM ALL

Bender, a broken-down old woman in her nineties, was living in a rooming house in Los Angeles. Like all other reports before, however, it proved false.

What really happened to the Benders remained a secret until 1936, when the last of the eight men who stood on the banks of the creek that night and took oath of silence died. On his deathbed the old man told a strange story to his son, who afterwards revealed it to the world.

When Colonel York found the stickpin in the yard, he rode immediately back to Thayer. When he related his story to two of the natives, they realized at once why the trails of so many strangers leading through their city had vanished. They also realized that none of their bodies had ever been found and arrest of the Benders would mean only strong denial. Without evidence there would be no prosecution.

Quietly, five other citizens were consulted. After serious consideration of the facts, it was agreed among the eight men that there was no use to report it to the authorities. Grimly they mounted their horses, and with a tall merchant in the lead, whose fury was rising rapidly against the family, they rode to the Bender nest.

It was dark when they arrived. Four of the group stationed themselves at the rear of the house to cut off any attempt to escape. The leader and the others approached the front door.

Their presence had already been discovered. Inside the house there was a flurry of excitement. Without knocking, the leader threw himself against the door, smashing it open.

PRAIRIE
VAMPIRE

As they entered, they covered the Benders with their rifles and six-shooters.

Kate stood near the curtain, her face devilish in the lamplight. In one hand she held a long knife. Behind her stood old man Bender. Instead of a Bible he held the heavy blacksmith hammer. John Bender wasn't in sight. The old lady, cursing violently, her face white with rage, leaped behind the counter and seized a shotgun. At that moment the other four men entered the back door and ordered her to drop the weapon. Old man Bender and Kate were seized and disarmed, and the moronic John, cursing and slobbering, was dragged from the dirty kitchen. All four refused to reveal the whereabouts of the body of Doctor York.

"You'll never find him!" Kate yelled. "You'll never find any of them!"

Her confession enraged the possemen. Already the leader had noticed bloodstains on the bottom of the curtain. Traces in the dust on the floor showed that the kitchen stove had been moved recently. They shoved it aside and discovered the trap door. They opened it and stepped back as the sickening stench arose. One of the men lighted a lantern and lowered it on a piece of cord. What they saw nearly turned them sick. The floor of the hole was caked with several inches of human blood.

The leader swung back to Kate. "For the last time," he demanded, "where is the body of Doctor York?"

"You'll never find it!" the murderess screamed again.

The leader nodded to his men. They seized the four

Benders and marched them into the night. On the banks of the Verdigris, at its junction with Fall River, the party halted. The Benders were given one more chance to reveal the location of the bodies. For reply, old man Bender and John whipped out revolvers which they somehow had managed to conceal in their clothing.

Posse guns roared and Bender and his son fell dead. Suddenly, vicious Kate Bender began begging for mercy. "Please don't kill my mother," she cried. "I'll tell everything."

"Where is Doctor York?"

"In the orchard," Kate confessed. "Look under the big cherry tree—"

"No, no!" yelled the old woman. "Don't tell them, Katie. Let them kill me!"

Savagely she tore free of the men who held her and snatched the pistol from the hand of her dead husband. The posse guns roared again. The old woman sank to the ground, her shots going wild into the night.

Kate screamed. She jerked a concealed knife from her bodice and sprang upon the leader in all her fury. Another bullet from a posseman's gun killed her.

The eight men stared down at the bodies of the murdering family. They had avenged the death of Doctor York and every other victim of their diabolical plot. They had also taken the law into their own hands, which caused them to kneel together and take the oath of secrecy. On the Bender farm, in the old well twenty feet deep, they tossed the four bodies and filled the shaft with rock and debris. Then they set about to effect an explanation for the strange disappearance of the family.

They hitched the Benders' team to the wagon. In the house two of the men dressed in the clothing of Kate Bender and her mother. Two others, who were about the ages of old William Bender and his son, drove them to Thayer, where the team and wagon had been found abandoned.

The train was due in a few minutes. The quartet hurried to the station and purchased tickets for Humboldt.[6] The ticket agent, a new man in the country, later described his customers as the Benders, and it was verified that they had boarded the train.

But when the four reached Chanute,[7] the next city, they had simply got off the train and returned to their homes. For sixty-three years the secret lay buried in their hearts and at the bottom of the old well.

6. *Ibid.*, p. 478.
7. *Ibid.*

CHAPTER V

Shadow of Billy the Kid

HENDRY BROWN

Civilization rolled westward behind the vanguard of soldier, scout, and plainsman. As the railroad thrust its twin ribbons of steel across the Kansas prairies a series of small towns mushroomed overnight. Texas cowboys coming up the trail with tens of thousands of longhorns—tired, dirty, and lonesome—craved every kind of pleasure their money could buy. When they had disposed of their herds, they swept down on the towns, spoiling for action, and got plenty of it. In Abilene, the first of these railhead capitals, saloons lined the street on both sides. Gamblers and dancehall girls relieved the free and easy cowboys of their loose change. Differences were settled with the six-shooter. Those who lost their arguments were laid to rest in Boothill.[1]

1. Joseph G. McCoy, *Historic Sketches of the Cattle Trade of the West and Southwest*, pp. 138–9.

There were no wilder days in the West. Most of the towns lasted only one explosive season, then the railroad pushed on, another town was created with a similar setting, the great herds of Texas cattle shifted, and the booming, blatant, iniquitous pattern repeated—Newton, Ellsworth, Wichita, Dodge.[2] In the spring of 1880, the railroad extended south to the Indian border, and Caldwell, Kansas, became the hell-roaring terminus of the Chisholm Trail.

From Indian Territory, Texas, and No Man's Land poured the longhorn herds. Over the same routes bounced the Concord stagecoach, and long strings of freight wagons creaked under heavy loads consigned to the agencies of the Indian tribes. There was great excitement over opening Oklahoma to settlement, and soldiers assigned to the border and the "boomer" they had come to keep out of the "promised land" made the town their headquarters.[3] Caldwell became "Queen City of the Border."[4] It had outgrown Dodge; its saloons, dancehalls, and gambling houses did more business than Abilene. To this mad mass of humanity flocked the disreputables and criminal parasites. Robberies and killings became so frequent, decent citizens were afraid to walk the streets after dark.

George Flat was appointed marshal. He became capricious, overbearing, and, finally, a drunkard. As he walked home one night past an implement yard, ambush guns

2. Stuart N. Lake, *Wyatt Earp, Frontier Marshal,* p. 69.
3. Charles A. Siringo, *Riata and Spurs,* pp. 116–7.
4. *Ibid.,* p. 112.

riddled him with buckshot and bullets. Mike Meagher put on the star and was slain in a gun battle with the Talbot gang, who had come up the trail to take the town. George Jones, a business man of fine judgment and cool deliberation, took up where Meagher left off. One night he was summoned to the Red Light Dance Hall to arrest two drunken cowboys who were shooting heels off the girls' slippers. As he entered the establishment, a gunshot roared in the room, and George Jones died with a bullet in his brain and his blood spreading across the floor.[5]

It was a sacrifice of human life for the officials to name a man to preserve law and order. The common fare was "a dead marshal for breakfast," and when the lone horseman rode into Caldwell one afternoon in the summer of 1882, "hilarity rode high, wide and handsome" and no man with a badge had been on the streets in three weeks.[6]

The stranger attracted no more attention than hundreds of others who drifted in from the trails, except that he wore a white hat, the brim of which was much narrower than that worn by most cowboys. He was a small, slender man, almost bony. But his square-set jaw had a bulldog appearance and he carried two ivory-handled Colts tied low on his hips and a well-worn Winchester on his saddle. Both horse and rider were covered with dust, for they had traveled far—all the way from Old Tascosa.

He stopped at the hitch-rail in front of the Golden Wedding saloon just north of Hubble's General Store, and

5. Sam P. Ridings, *The Chisholm Trail*, pp. 490–1.
6. Owen P. White, *Lead and Likker*, p. 202.

went inside. Following the custom of patrons who sought no trouble, he deposited his pistols with the bartender. He inquired for the mayor of the town, and after being informed where he could find the chief executive, he surprised the crowd by walking out without buying a drink.

He stood, a few minutes later, in the mayor's office and told him: "I know a man who can handle the marshal's job in Caldwell."

The mayor's worried frown deepened. "Who is he?" he asked, doubtful. "When can he start?"

"I can take over right now," the stranger replied quietly.

The mayor was a big man. Staring at this mere lath of an individual from behind his desk, he thought the latter was making a joke of the town's dilemma. He arose to his full height, towering over the stranger, his face flushed.

"You don't look like the man to fill the bill—" he began, then paused abruptly.

The stranger's whitish-blue eyes had taken on a chilly glint. The muscles of his square jaw tightened.

"I didn't ask for any lip," he stated. His manner was almost surly. It was obvious also that he cared nothing for the display the official had made of his greater physique.

Slowly the mayor settled back into his chair. His anger faded in a grin of sly humor.

"All right," he agreed. "It's your funeral. What is your name?"

The stranger said simply: "Hendry Brown."

TOUGHEST OF
THEM ALL

The name meant nothing to the mayor. The crowd in the saloon had never heard of him. But all watched with interest when he returned for his guns, wearing the law badge.

One twangy-voiced gambler advised: "This is a bad town for lawmen, son. None has lasted more'n a week."

"That don't worry me," Brown replied. "I'll be on duty at six o'clock." Then he was gone.

As the doors flapped behind him, the gambler remarked to the crowd: "Well, boys, this one looks mild. I'm layin' bets he don't last one evenin'."

"Reckon you're bettin' on a cinch," opined one of the toughs, and the gang retired to the back room to arrange the details of what was to be a surprise party for Hendry Brown.

Meanwhile, the new marshal put up his horse and secured lodging for himself at the Texas House. That he had not been recognized was to his advantage. As he sat in his room with a good meal under his belt, cleaning and oiling his rifle and six-shooters, he hummed a little tune he had learned in a Mexican dance hall down in Fort Sumner, New Mexico.

Hendry Brown's nativity is not known. He never mentioned his family. The first historical record of him is in the late '70s when he appeared as a cowboy on John Chisum's South Springs Ranch, near Roswell, at the outbreak of active hostilities in the Lincoln County War.[7]

He had ridden stirrup to stirrup and fought shoulder

7. Sam P. Ridings, *The Chisholm Trail,* p. 493.

to shoulder with Billy the Kid in all his bloody glory.[8] He was with the Kid in the massacre at Agua Negra Spring on March 9, 1878, when Deputies Bill Morton and Frank Baker, who were their prisoners, were shot to death, and McCloskey, a companion of the Kid and Brown, was mysteriously slain when he tried to protect the hostages.[9] He rode alongside the Kid the day Sheriff William Brady and his deputy, George Hindman, were assassinated on the main street of Lincoln.[10] And in July, 1878, he and the Kid stood siege with a dozen hand-picked warriors of the Chisum-McSween clan in the home of Alexander McSween and battled more than seventy members of the L. G. Murphy faction for three days. The Kid ran the gauntlet of blazing guns, drawing the fire, enabling Brown and the others to escape in the night.[11]

After this, wherever the Kid went, there went Hendry Brown. When the Lincoln County War ended, he and the Kid, with three other members of the gang,[12] fled northeast up the Pecos valley, stealing some 125 horses and mares along the Bonito and around the Capitan Mountains, and running them into the Texas Panhandle as far east as Old Tascosa,[13] where again together they whooped off their profits drinking, gambling, and shooting at targets.[14]

8. Charles A. Siringo, *A Texas Cowboy, or Fifteen Years on the Hurricane Deck of a Spanish Pony*, p. 170.

9. Walter Noble Burns, *Saga of Billy the Kid*, p. 90.

10. George W. Coe, *Frontier Fighter*, pp. 57–8.

11. *Ibid.*, pp. 117–19.

12. John Middleton, Fred Waite, and Tom O'Folliard.

13. Emerson Hough, *The Story of the Outlaw*, p. 263.

14. John L. McCarty, *Maverick Town, the Story of Old Tascosa*, p. 79.

In fact, nearly every activity credited to Billy the Kid, from the time they joined forces until they parted at Old Tascosa, should have been credited as well to Hendry Brown. Nor was their separation due to any misunderstanding. On the contrary, they parted the best of friends.

Fred Waite and John Middleton wanted to quit the outlaw life and went to Indian Territory. The Kid and O'Folliard returned to their old haunts between Lincoln and Fort Sumner, were joined by Tom Pickett, Billy Wilson, Dave Rudabaugh, Charlie Bowdre, and others, and began rustling cattle from ranges as far east as the Canadian and selling them in butcher shops in the mining camp of White Oaks and at Las Vegas.[15] And Brown, having heard much of the wide open trail towns of Kansas, rode north to see how tough they really were. It would have been a jolt to the mayor to have known the turbulent past of the man he had just hired; and the party being planned by the "reception committee" down at the saloon more than likely would have been canceled.

The surprise planned for Hendry Brown was the same crude scheme which, up to now, had proven very effective. One man would tip the gang the instant the new marshal left his room to begin his night tour of duty; a second would cut loose with a series of wolf-calls and start firing his pistol into the already bullet-punctured ceiling; and when Brown rushed inside to make an arrest, still two other toughs would run interference. Brown could either check

15. *Ibid.*, pp. 83–4.

in his badge and hightail or cash his chips. They didn't care which.

Promptly at six o'clock Brown left the Texas House. The moment he stepped into the street he sensed something was afoot. Down at the Golden Wedding the yelling and shooting began.

Tense and alert, Brown hurried toward the saloon. But he didn't rush inside, as the gang had planned. Instead, he eased through the doors, his practised eyes taking in the situation at a glance. His attention, without seeming to be, was on every man in the room except the one creating the disturbance. He waited until the offender had emptied his pistol, then approached him. Off to the side he saw the two toughs reach for their weapons. Two shots roared in the room, but both came from Hendry Brown's gun, and the pair fell dead in their tracks. Then Brown thumped the bewildered lawbreaker across the head with his still-smoking six-shooter, disarmed him, and locked on the handcuffs.

"If any more of you hombres get any hell-raisin' ideas, I'll be down at my office!" he informed the astounded patrons, and hustled his first prisoner off to jail.

Caldwell was dazed. Soberly they buried Brown's first victims, and things quieted down for a week. Then they snapped out of it.

A minstrel show was coming to town. Not that the sporting element was interested in a minstrel show, but there was going to be a parade. According to the advance billing, the troupe would arrive by train and march down the street to the Opera House, led by a brass band and wearing plug hats. What an opportunity for the trigger experts of Caldwell to demonstrate their prowess!

The pistoleers polished their weapons. The frock-coated gamblers made up a pot to be paid to the man who "shot the most hats off the most niggers." But on the morning that the troupe arrived the plan leaked out, and the mayor advised the manager of the show to call off the procession. It was the only sensible thing to do under the circumstances, but when Hendry Brown heard that the parade had been canceled, he hurried to the mayor's office.

"People are packed on both sides of the street, waitin'. Caldwell's goin' to see a parade!" he told the mayor. To the show manager, he said: "Tell them minstrels to do their stuff. If anybody interferes, they'll answer to me!"

The parade proceeded as scheduled. When the first cowboy drew his pistol and shot off one of the Negro's hats, Brown sent a bullet ripping into the boardwalk between his toes. Approaching the cowboy quickly and shoving the muzzle of his six-shooter close to his face, he said:

"Now dance, damn you, dance! Show these niggers a new buck and wing step!"

The cowboy tried, but the marshal wasn't satisfied. "You can't dance," he said in disgust. "Maybe you can run!"

The cowboy fled, but Hendry's next bullet brought him down. While he lay moaning in the street, the marshal faced the rest of the gang. "Any more of you hombres don't know it's against the law to discharge firearms in a public place?"

SHADOW OF
BILLY THE KID

The parade continued without further trouble.

The city council authorized Brown to appoint one deputy. He chose a tall, stalwart Texan named Ben Wheeler.

The pair made a comical sight walking down the street together. Brown appeared much smaller, almost insignificant, alongside the huge, wide-shouldered Wheeler. But what he lacked in size Brown, like his old sidekick, Billy the Kid, made up in fast guns and cold nerve. He killed several men during his first few months in office. He enforced the law rigidly. Those who carried guns to the city deposited them at the limits or carried them, muzzles reversed, to the nearest checking place. He set after the lawless with such vigor that they either put up or shut up or left town. So pleased was the council with this deliverance of their cattle city that they presented Brown with a gold-mounted Winchester rifle and a gold-mounted saddle, and gave Wheeler a saddle mounted with silver.[16]

From that day, the remainder of Hendry Brown's career as Caldwell's marshal reveals no record of another killing.

The lawless had been subdued. The roaring railhead had settled down to a peace-loving community. But Hendry Brown had tamed it too well.

There was nothing to do, no one to shoot at, no activity. He grew lonesome for the excitement of the old days when he had ridden knee to knee with the Kid in the Lincoln County War and stole horses along the Bonito and around the Capitans. And, suddenly, a situation far more terrifying

16. Sam P. Ridings, *The Chisholm Trail,* pp. 495–6.

to the citizens than the tough element had been, gripped the city.

People found themselves being slugged and robbed in alleys and out-of-way places. A secret organization infested the community. And, strangely, Brown and Deputy Wheeler were unable to put a finger on the persons responsible. They were always working on the opposite side of town when the offenses were committed. Not until May 1, 1884, was the organization fully exposed.

The evening before, Hendry Brown and Ben Wheeler rode south toward the Cherokee Outlet, presumably in search of horse thieves. Outside of town they circled back, stopped at a cow camp on the T5 range and picked up two cowboys, named William Smith and John Wesley. Early the next morning, the quartet rode through a drizzling rain into Medicine Lodge, fifty miles northwest of Caldwell, and dismounted in front of the Medicine Valley Bank. While Smith held the horses, Brown, Wheeler, and Wesley hurried inside.

E. Wylie Payne, the president, and Cashier George Geppert were on duty. Payne recognized Hendry Brown and asked the marshal what he could do for them.

"Both of you can stick up your hands!" Brown replied.

The cashier complied, but Payne reached for a gun. Brown promptly shot him dead. Geppert turned the knob which locked the vault, and Ben Wheeler killed the cashier. Scooping up what money was available, the trio fled to their horses.

The shooting aroused the citizens. A dozen men rushed

up the street, firing upon Smith. Smith was barely able to hold his own until his companions burst from the bank. They shot their way clear and escaped from town with a posse in pursuit.

They headed southwest and crossed Medicine River. Wheeler's mount bogged down in the quicksand and he had to abandon it. This left the deputy and one of the cowboys riding one horse.

The delay placed the posse close on their heels. They cut southeast into the Gypsum Hills, and, being unfamiliar with the country, rode into a blind canyon.

The posse closed in. The fugitives quit their horses and fought back on foot until they stood waist deep in water that had filled the recess. Hopelessly trapped and outnumbered, the four men surrendered.

They were returned to Medicine Lodge and placed in jail. From Caldwell flocked irate citizens who had been slugged and robbed. They joined others in Medicine Lodge incensed with the brutal slayings of the two popular bank officials. At midnight a mob broke into the jail and overpowered the guards.

Brown rushed from the door in a desperate bid for his life. A charge of buckshot struck him in the back and he died before he had run a dozen yards. Wheeler ran out at the same time, fleeing in the opposite direction. A gun blasted at him from close range, setting fire to his shirt. The blaze became the target for other guns, and Wheeler fell, badly wounded. Smith and Wesley had no chance to escape. The mob seized and dragged them from the jail.

The next morning their bodies, together with Wheeler's, hung from a limb of a big elm a half mile east of Medicine Lodge.

Thus ended the career of Hendry Brown, whose energy and ability had made him, for a short while, a useful citizen. Had he respected the principles he had so capably upheld, he might well have been greater than Bill Tilghman, of Oklahoma, Hickok, of Abilene; Bat Masterson and Wyatt Earp, of Dodge and Wichita; or even Pat Garrett, who, finally, downed his old pal, the Kid.

CHAPTER VI

Coyote Kind

BOB OLLINGER

Some years ago, Emerson Hough wrote: "Throughout the West there are two sorts wolves—the coyote and the gray wolf. Either will kill, but both are lovers of blood. One is yellow at heart, and the other is game all the way through. In outward appearance both are wolves, and in appearance they sometimes grade toward each other so closely that it is hard to determine the species. The gray wolf is a warrior and is respected. The coyote is a sneak and a murderer, and his name is a term of reproach throughout the West." [1]

Hough was drawing the difference between the actual Western bad man and the imitation desperado. The real bad man, he said, was an evolution, the imitation bad man an instantaneous creation. [2] Both were killers. It was difficult to tell them apart by their looks. Usually the bogus

1. Emerson Hough, *The Story of the Outlaw*, pp. 20–1.
2. *Ibid.*, p. 14.

bad man acted and dressed like a present-day movie and fiction villain. He was coarse-looking, swashbuckling, overdid the wearing of his apparel and weapons, was profusely boisterous and profane, and loved a reputation. Seldom, if ever, after looking and acting the part for a while, did he get wise to himself and vanish from the scene voluntarily. He discovered how easily he could terrify the population of a whole community. Often his base activities were exalted in the public eye. Then, as today, he was idolized by large numbers of maudlin individuals. He took himself seriously until he ran up against some quiet voiced little fellow who meant the few words he said. Either he "got dusted on both sides" and began to respect the peace and dignity of the community or he was carried away feet first to Boothill. Meanwhile, he reveled in the belief that he really was "bad."

Bob Ollinger was an excellent example. Ollinger, who served the latter part of his "bad man" career as deputy under Sheriff Pat Garrett, was probably the most typical imitation desperado the West has ever known.

He already had gained his reputation as a killer years before he came to Lincoln County, New Mexico, and joined the L. G. Murphy forces against the combine of John Chisum and Alexander McSween, represented by the band of gun warriors under the leadership of Billy the Kid, in the Lincoln County War. But he had gained it without standing the severe test, with no danger for himself. He had slain three victims, treacherously and brutally.

While marshal of Seven Rivers, Ollinger was offended

in some small way by an old friend, Juan Chavez. He kept up a show of friendship, nursing the grudge secretly. One day the two met on the street. "Hello, Chavez." Ollinger smiled in good humor. Chavez extended his hand in greeting. Ollinger seized it with his left. With his right he drew his revolver and fired. Chavez dropped dead at his feet.[3]

Ollinger's second victim was a man named John Hill. History does not record the details of this killing. The facts available show that Hill was shot in the back without warning, with no chance to defend himself.[4]

A short time later, Ollinger went with Deputy Sheriff Pierce to serve a misdemeanor warrant on a man named Bob Jones. Rumor had it that there was bad blood between Jones and Ollinger and that Ollinger was afraid of him. In any event, the warrant had been issued for a minor offense and Ollinger had volunteered his assistance in making the arrest. Jones surrendered peaceably; and, seconds later, while he stood unarmed and defenseless in Pierce's custody, Ollinger drew his six-shooter and fired three bullets into his body. The crime was unprovoked and inexcusable. But it satiated the craving of Ollinger's bloodthirsty soul and disposed of another man he hated.[5]

Ollinger's personal appearance was enough to capture the fancy of the adolescent, the greenhorn, and others who didn't know better. Physically, he was powerful,

3. Walter Noble Burns, *The Saga of Billy the Kid,* p. 225.
4. *Ibid.*
5. *Ibid.,* pp. 225–6.

broad-shouldered, a man about forty, red-faced and black-eyed. His raven hair flowed down over his shoulders after the manner of Wild Bill Hickok. His dress was picturesque. He wore a buckskin hunting coat, fringed and elaborately designed in colored beads and porcupine quills like those of the early-day scouts and Indian fighters. Two six-shooters and a long-bladed knife, similar to the Bowie, always hung from a wide cartridge belt about his waist.

Thus superbly garnished, and armed to the teeth, his sombrero cocked jauntily to one side and his pants stuffed into the tops of gaily embroidered boots, he would parade down the street, dramatizing himself and performing spectacular feats like picking insects off a twig or limb with a spew of tobacco juice, demonstrating the swiftness of his draw, or driving his knife into a tree or board with such velocity that it would stick deep with a thud and quiver.[6] In larger towns, like Santa Fe and Las Vegas, he would swagger through the streets, followed by crowds of small boys, creating a fury of excitement. Afterward he would lounge in the public square, basking in the awe he had inspired, spreading his long hair down his back and nonchalantly picking his teeth with his ten-inch blade while the populace gaped.[7]

Sheriff Pat Garrett held no illusions about Ollinger. Excusing his appointment, he said: "Deputies in these dangerous times are difficult to get." A short while after he was made deputy, Ollinger tried to kill another man in cold

6. George D. Hendricks, *The Bad Man of the West*, p. 96.
7. Emerson Hough, *The Story of the Outlaw*, p. 19.

blood after the latter had thrown down his gun and surrendered to Garrett. "When I brought the Mexican out of
the ditch where he was hiding," Garrett said, explaining
later what happened, "Ollinger came running toward us,
his six-shooter cocked in his hand and his long hair flying
in the wind. I never saw so devilish a look on any human
being's face. The Mexican leaped behind me, but Ollinger
circled around trying to get at him. I told Bob to leave him
alone, but he paid me no mind and dodged around again
in an effort to get a shot. Finally I pointed my gun in his
face and told him I would kill him if he did not stop. That
brought him to his senses."

Ollinger had made numerous threats against Billy the
Kid. Neither of the pair placed any value on human life.
They differed in that the Kid was willing to risk his own.
In the Lincoln County War, Billy the Kid stole the lime-
light. Fighting on the opposite side made him Ollinger's
natural enemy. But the deputy's deadly hatred for the Kid
grew from the death of Bob Beckwith,[8] Ollinger's closest
friend, whom the Kid killed in the fight between the two
factions in Lincoln.[9] After the Kid was captured and sentenced to hang for the murder of Sheriff William Brady,
Ollinger bid for, and was granted, the privilege of guard-
ing him in jail during the two weeks preceding his execution.

Hardly an hour passed during the long wait that Ollinger did not throw sarcastic remarks at the Kid, ridiculed

8. *Ibid.*, p. 269.
9. George W. Coe, *Frontier Fighter*, p. 118.

him and cursed him to his face, and on three occasions menaced him with a sawed-off double-barreled shotgun. Quiet and small, blond-haired, blue-eyed, the Kid took Ollinger's jibes and silently vowed revenge. On the evening of April 28, 1881, before he was to be hanged on May 13th, he caught Jailer James W. Bell unawares as he was returning the Kid from a privy in the back yard, struck Bell over the head with his shackles and seized his revolver, killing him with it.[10] Ollinger, who had left the Kid alone with Bell while he took the other prisoners to a cafe across the street,[11] heard the shot and hurried toward the corner of the courthouse. He had left his shotgun in Garrett's office, and he circled the building to come up the stairs at the back. Meanwhile the Kid had gotten rid of his handcuffs and leg irons. As he passed through the room he grabbed up the weapon. He saw Ollinger coming at a running walk, and, as the deputy neared the corner of the building, a cigar in his mouth, the Kid stepped to the east window on the balcony.

"Hello, old fellow!" he called pleasantly.

When Ollinger looked up, the outlaw grinned and pulled the trigger. The impact of the blast drove Ollinger's cigar down his throat and tore off the top of his head. He sprawled backward in the dust. The Kid leaped outside. Again he raised Ollinger's shotgun and emptied the other barrel into the dead deputy. Then he broke the weapon

10. Emerson Hough, *The Story of the Outlaw*, p. 269.
11. J. W. Hendron, *The Story of Billy the Kid, New Mexico's Number One Desperado*, p. 25.

COYOTE
KIND

over the balcony railing, and as he came down the stairs, angrily threw it across the body, saying: "Take that, you son of a bitch. You will never follow me with that gun again." [12] Then he mounted a horse and rode away.

Sheriff Garrett was at White Oaks ordering the lumber to be used in erecting Billy the Kid's gallows when he received word of the Kid's escape and Ollinger's death. The lumber later was used to make a coffin for his deputy.[13]

12. Charles A. Siringo, *A Texas Cowboy, or Fifteen Years on the Hurricane Deck of a Spanish Pony,* p. 174.

13. J. W. Hendron, *The Story of Billy the Kid, New Mexico's Number One Desperado,* p. 27.

CHAPTER VII

Gun-Lawyer of the Plains

TEMPLE HOUSTON

The perils of the West were as nothing compared to its attractions. On the wild, raw frontier, where everybody was on their own conduct, men found wide opportunity to exploit their personalities and acquire fame and unique reputations. The rule applied even in the formal professions. Lawyers became notorious for their traits and actions.

Temple Houston, son of the Texas liberator, was incomparably the most singularly fascinating of them all.

He was six feet two inches in height, wore the typical dress of a Southern planter—long, flowing hair and small, high-heeled boots drawn over the lower ends of his pantaloons. In his long coat, a broad-brimmed hat, and, generally, with one or more pistols protruding from his hip pockets, he presented a spectacle. He was conspicuous not only in his dress. He had great gifts and strong passions.

He was an eloquent orator and behind his eloquence lay the keen reasoning of a brilliant mind. His every word and act was dramatic in the extreme. Frank and engaging, he won renown in politics in the state of his nativity and for nearly a quarter century was the Southwest's best known criminal lawyer. He defended more criminals than any other man in his day and time. His characteristic greeting to officials when they came to court was: "Have you come out to the hangin'?"

Furthermore, he took no back seat to the gun-artists of the era. His numerous affrays proved his ability with a six-shooter, and his manner of execution showed he was afraid of no living man.

The empire he held in thrall stretched from Brazoria County, Texas, to the Panhandle, and at the time of his death had grown to include the whole western half of that progressive country known as Oklahoma Territory, then clamoring for statehood honors. He attended all the courts in the western counties and took some part in most of the cases and all the important ones.

He was little more than a babe in arms in February, 1861,[1] when the Secession Convention of Texas took the governorship away from his father.[2] Deprived of his office, General Sam Houston went first to his old home at Independence, but in a little while moved to another home at Huntsville,[3] where he died July 26, 1863.

1. Marquis James, *The Raven, A Biography of Sam Houston*, p. 431.
2. *Ibid.*, pp. 405–12.
3. *Ibid.*, p. 418.

In the latter part of 1864, when Temple was nearly five, his mother moved the family back to Independence. She died when he was seven.

Temple lived with relatives until he was thirteen, then began riding the ranges of the Lone Star State as a cowboy. Following the lead of his adventuresome spirit, he drove a longhorn herd to Bismarck, North Dakota, then hired out as a clerk on a steamer and took a trip down the Mississippi to New Orleans. His father's political friends soon secured a position for the boy as a page in the United States Senate, and during his four years in Washington, Temple studied law, and was admitted to the Texas bar at the age of nineteen. He opened an office in Brazoria County, and soon attracted such wide attention with his masterful handling of criminal cases that the voters placed in his hands the job of bringing the numerous law violators of the locality to the bar of justice. When the legislature created a new court for the Texas Panhandle district, Temple Houston applied for and won the appointment as first district attorney before he had reached his twenty-first birthday.[4]

He found his new office no bed of roses. Law and order had not become fashionable in the Panhandle, and the country was a mecca for the outlaw, the gunman, and others of their ilk.

Most of the towns in the district were small. Tascosa was a center of supplies for the big cattle ranches, and

4. Joseph B. Thoburn and Muriel H. Wright, *Oklahoma, a History of the State and Its People,* pp. 442-3.

was patronized by other people moving across the Indian and cattle trails to the west. A large number of gamblers, cutthroats, thieves, and painted women infested its environs as the result of a general cleanup at Mobeetie by Captain G. W. Arrington, of the Texas Rangers.[5] Roundup and trail-herd cowboys made it their headquarters for relaxation. This was after the Lincoln County War, when Billy the Kid and his gang were hanging around, racing and trading stolen horses and shooting at targets. Temple Houston pitted his skill against the best of them, and outshot United States Marshal Bat Masterson and Billy the Kid in a money match which drew explosive applause from the audience and congratulations from the Kid himself.[6] After this, Houston experienced little difficulty encouraging obedience of the law.

With nine other counties attached for judicial purposes, Tascosa became the most important town in that part of the West, and center of a judicial empire. Court was held twice a year and lasted two weeks. The semiannual meeting was a gala occasion. All work in the region was suspended as people flocked in from everywhere. Horse races, spelling bees, and many other such events were staged for added entertainment. Houston spiced the affair with his own personal sideshow. He let his raven-black hair grow until it reached his shoulders. He dressed in flashy clothes, often wore a beautiful white hat, and used courtly,

5. J. Evetts Haley, *Charles Goodnight, Cowman and Plainsman*, pp. 356–7.

6. John L. McCarty, *Maverick Town, the Story of Old Tascosa*, p. 79.

graceful manners. He became a favorite of the ladies, popular with the men, and went into his job energetically and made a good prosecutor.[7]

But Tascosa's importance as a court center soon faded. Other counties attached to Oldham began to organize themselves, major cases became mostly civil and land suits, and court sessions attracted only the few people involved.[8] Such humdrum activity was not for Temple Houston.

When A. L. Matlock, of Montague, who had been representing that region in the state senate, stepped down, Temple ran for that office and was elected. The Panhandle district, at that time comprising fifty-six counties, won him an advanced and important position in the senate. He became a statesman of power and influence, was returned to office for a second term in 1886, and, at the dedication of the capital in 1888, he was chosen to deliver the dedicatory address.

There was an immense crowd in Austin for the occasion. People swarmed over the capital grounds to hear his speech, and the newspapers pronounced it "an able and most worthy address from a worthy son of a most distinguished sire." To these rough and sympathetic people he was a marvel. His words brought tears to their eyes. Had Temple Houston so desired, Texas would have placed him in the Senate of the United States.

But the opening of the Cherokee Outlet, in Oklahoma,

7. *Ibid.*, pp. 176–7.
8. *Ibid.*

offered new worlds to conquer. Here was an opportunity for leadership in the political circles of a rapidly developing state, as much to his liking as the old days when he had first come to Tascosa and matched shots with Bat Masterson and Billy the Kid. His second senatorial term having ended, Houston went to Woodward and opened a law office in 1893.[9]

He had an even more hectic career in Oklahoma. He first attracted territory-wide attention by shooting up a gambling house in Guthrie and putting all its occupants to flight because he saw a small boy lose all his money.[10]

Shortly afterwards he took one of his most famous cases. At Cheyenne, Red Tom, a Texas cowboy, had killed an Indian. The cowboy had come to town looking for trouble. He followed his victim around all evening. When the Indian entered a restaurant and purchased a cup of coffee, Red Tom followed him inside and took it away from him. Wanting no trouble and only to get away from the cowboy, the Indian got in his wagon and drove out of town. Red Tom followed and killed him, then returned to Cheyenne, saying: "If you find an Indian out there with a bullet in his head, he is my Indian."

It was cold-blooded murder. To prevent a lynching, the sheriff spirited Red Tom to El Reno, where he went on trial. It was a clear case for the prosecution. Houston offered no evidence in the cowboy's defense. But the trial was before a Texas jury, and every Texan admired

9. The *Beaver Herald*, March 14, 1893.
10. *Oklahoma City Times Journal*, Dec. 27, 1893.

Houston. It was Houston's custom to first get a Texas jury angry.

Nearly every member was familar with the Cheyenne-Arapaho outbreaks.

Houston worked upon the prejudices of the people of the country against the Indians. He made an eloquent address and "twined it with garlands of metaphor." At a moment when the temper of the jury was at fever pitch, he shouted:

"Not one of you but remembers the time when, with drawn bow and lifted lance, the Indians of the same tribe, by the light of your burning homes, were murdering your wives and children. Mercy, eh! Where was mercy then?"

The jury, within a few minutes, brought in a verdict of acquittal for Red Tom.

Once in commenting on the testimony of a Negro, Houston declared: "He sat there manufacturing perjury as gaily as a mocking bird ever sang his lay." [11]

Often Houston appeared in the courtroom in remarkable raiment. One day at Taloga he strode in before Judge John H. Burford wearing highly embroidered cloth slippers and a neck scarf made of a mammoth rattlesnake skin. The idea of a snake being tied around a man's neck worried Judge Burford, and, as the trial progressed, he became very nervous. Finally he remarked: "If the distinguished counsel will permit, I wish to say that rattlesnakes

11. *Guthrie Daily Leader,* Aug. 21, 1894, "Hon. Temple Houston, of Woodward, the son of General Sam Houston of Texas fame, is known as 'the silver tongued orator of Oklahoma.' "

or anything resembling them give me the shivers and distract my attention from the business at hand. The gentleman from Woodward will oblige the court by returning after dinner without his rattlesnake-skin cravat."

When Houston came back after dinner, he was smiling and wearing a gorgeous green tie that would have enthused an Irishman.

Another of his unique methods of impressing a jury was demonstrated, while defending a cowboy on a murder charge, by showing that his client had feared the reputation of his victim as a quick-drawing gunman, and because of this fear, had shot before the latter had time to draw.

"Gentlemen of the jury," Houston said, "this man had a gunman's reputation while my client here is an ordinary, hard-working citizen like yourselves, little experienced in the use of firearms. Do you have any idea how little chance any of you would stand in the face of the lightning draw of a gun-artist? Do you have any idea what speed this dead man possessed? Why—!" he shouted and, before the jurymen could blink their eyes, Houston whipped a .45 from his pocket and pointed it at the jury box. He shot six times rapidly, while the jury ducked for cover and the judge leaped from his rostrum and headed through the nearest door. When the excitement was over, and the judge had crawled back to his bench and the jurymen had timidly settled back in their box, Houston offered his sincere apologies. "Your honor, you need not have been afraid. My cartridges were all blanks. It was only necessary that I show you what little chance an ordinary man, like my client, would have had with that gunman."

Although such eccentric acts brought Temple Houston a great deal of notoriety, his ability as a lawyer was not underestimated. His reputation as a fighter made it easy for him to intimidate opposing counsel, and he precipitated many bitter clashes in the territorial courts.

Although he was acquitted of the charge,[12] there is little doubt that he killed Ed Jennings, brother of John and Al Jennings, of the law firm of Jennings & Jennings, of Woodward. The two had clashed over numerous points of a case in court. The lie was passed, guns were drawn, and a dozen men had rushed to the pair to separate them. The court rebuked the two attorneys and they apologized. But that evening, while Houston was standing with an old friend and ex-sheriff Jack Love at a local bar, Ed and John Jennings entered. Revolvers appeared simultaneously and the shooting began. All engaged in a running, dodging fight except Houston. The big lawyer stood up straight and emptied his revolver without twitching a muscle. When the smoke cleared, Ed Jennings was dead and John had an arm shot away.[13]

Al Jennings grew bitter about the acquittal. He cursed the court and swore he would kill Temple Houston.[14] He went to Houston's home one night to shoot him through the window as he sat by a lamp, reading. As he raised his

---

12. *The South and West,* May 21, 1896.
13. *Oklahoma City Times Journal,* Oct. 10, 1895.
14. Evett Dumas Nix, *Oklahombres,* pp. 246–7.

rifle, Houston's wife passed between him and the window. Jennings stated afterwards he hadn't the heart to kill him before his family. Once Houston and Jennings happened to be in Guthrie at the same time. Bantz Gano, a hotel clerk, happened to put the two men in adjoining rooms. There was consternation when it was learned what he had done. To avoid trouble, Jennings was rushed to another hotel. For months the killing of Houston or Jennings, one by the other, was expected at any time, and such would probably have occurred had not Al Jennings been convicted of train robbery and sentenced to the penitentiary.

The speech for which Temple Houston is best remembered was made in May, 1899, in Judge John H. Burford's court in defense of a fallen woman, Minnie Stacey. All sorts of cases were being tried in the Woodward court in those days—wrangles over land titles, thefts, damages, shooting scrapes. Temple was always around, taking part in first one case and then another. When the woman was brought before the court, charged with plying her vocation and running a bawdy house, Houston was sitting in the courtroom unoccupied, listening to the procedure. When the judge learned that the woman had no counsel, he appointed Houston to defend her.

Houston talked with the woman a short time, then appeared for trial. According to newspaper reports of the time, exposure had impaired his voice. The court and jury were surprised when he began talking to them only in a calm, conversational tone.

After briefly reviewing the legal questions involved and

discussing the evidence the prosecution had presented, Temple Houston rose to his feet. He leaned over the jury box until he could almost touch each man on the shoulder and in the same low, appealing voice closed his address with the following words:

"Gentlemen: You have heard with what cold cruelty the prosecution referred to the sins of this woman, as if her condition were of her own preference. The evidence has painted you a picture of her life and surroundings.

"Do you think that they were of her own choosing? Do you think that she willingly embraced a life so revolting and horrible? Ah, no! Gentlemen, one of our sex was the author of her ruin, more to blame than she.

"Then let us judge her gently. What could be more pathetic than the spectacle she presents? An immortal soul in ruin—where the star of purity once glittered on her girlish brow, burning shame has set its seal forever; and only a moment ago they reproved her of the depths to which she has sunk, the company she kept and the life she led. Now, what is left for her? Where can she go and her sin not pursue her?

"Gentlemen, the very promises of God are denied her. He said, 'Come unto me all ye that labor and are heavy laden and I will give you rest.' She has indeed labored and is heavy laden, but if at this instant she were to kneel down before us all and confess her Redeemer and beseech His tender mercies, where is the church that would receive her? And even if they accepted her, when she passed the portals to worship and claim her rest, scorn and mockery would greet her and those she met would gather around them their skirts closely to avoid the pollution of her touch. Would you tell me a single employment where she can realize: 'Give us this day our daily bread?'

"Our sex wrecked her once pure life—her own sex shrink from her as they would the pestilence. Society has reared its relentless walls against her and only in the friendly shelter of the grace can her betrayed and broken heart find the Redeemer's promised rest. They told you of her assumed names, as fleeting as the shadows on the walls; of her sins, her habits, but they never told you of her sorrows, and who shall tell what her heart, sinful though it may be, now feels?

"When the remembered voices of mother and sisters whom she must see no more on this earth fall like music on her erring soul and she prays God that she could only return, and must not, no, not in this life, for the seducer has destroyed her soul. You know the story of the prodigal son, but he was a son. He was one of us, like her destroyer; but for the prodigal daughter there is no return. Were she with her wasted form and bleeding feet to drag herself back to home, she, the fallen and lost, what would be her welcome?

"Oh, consider this when you come to decide her guilt, for she is before us and we must judge her. They sneer and scoff at her. One should respect her grief, and I tell you, there reigns over her penitent and chastened spirit a desolation now that none, no, none but the searchers of all hearts can ever know.

TOUGHEST OF
THEM ALL

"None of us utterly is evil, and I remember when the Saffron Scourge swept over the city of Memphis in 1878, a courtesan there opened wide her doors of her gilded palace of sin to admit the sufferers; and when the scythe of the reaper swung fast and pitiless she was angelic in her ministering. Death called her in the midst of her mercies and she went to join those she tried to save. She, like those the Lord forgave, was a sinner, and yet I believe that in the day of reckoning her judgment will be lighter than those who prosecute and seek to drive off the earth such poor unfortunates as she whom you are to judge.

"They wish to fine this woman and make her leave. They wish to wring from the wages of her shame the price of this meditated injustice; to take from her the little money she might have; and God knows, gentlemen, it came hard enough. The old Jewish law told you that the price of a dog, nor the hire of such as she, should come within the house of the Lord, and I say unto you that our justice, fitly symbolized by a woman's form, does not ask that you add aught to the woes of this unhappy one who only asks at your hands the pitiful privilege of being left alone.

"The Master while on earth, while He spoke in wrath and rebuke to the kings and rulers, never reproached one of these. One he forgave; another he acquitted. You remember both, and now looking upon this friendless outcast, if any of us can say unto her, 'I am holier than thou,' in the respect with which she is charged with sinning, who is he?

"The Jews who brought the woman before the Savior

GUN-LAWYER
OF THE PLAINS

90

have been held up to the execration of the world for 2,000 years. I always respected them. A man who will yield to the reproaches of his conscience as they did has the elements of good in him, but the modern hypocrite has no such compunction.

"If the prosecutors of this woman whom you are trying had but brought her before the Savior they would have accepted his challenge and each one gathered a rock and stoned her in the twinkling of an eye.

"No, gentlemen, do as your Master did twice under the very circumstances that surround you. Tell her to go in peace."

The jury acquitted her as soon as they could reach their room.

Houston's extemporaneous speech in the woman's defense was so appealing that, afterwards, the court's stenographer was besieged with requests. Thousands of copies of the oration were printed and circulated. In his later years, Houston prepared beautiful lectures and delivered them in churches throughout the territory. In 1897, he was invited by the state of Tennessee, where his father was once governor, to deliver the centennial address at the opening of the Tennessee exposition at Nashville.[15]

Houston's principal fault was his bulldog stubbornness. When he decided a thing was right he decided upon it with all his soul. He seldom mentioned the name of his father. It was said that a sure way to incur his displeasure was to speak of him as the son of the hero of San Jacinto.

15. *The Indian Chieftain*, Feb. 11, 1897.

He did not wish to shine in the luster of his father's greatness. He believed that a man was only what he made himself; if a lion, he could fight his own battles; if a weakling, no rumor of distinguished lineage could make him strong.

Temple Houston died at Woodward, August 14, 1905. His activities and principles left an ineffaceable imprint upon the early history of the two states in which he lived.

CHAPTER VIII

Buckshot on the Brazos

THE MARLOWS

It was the bleak morning of December 17, 1888. The stage was set on the Brazos River, near Graham, in Young County, Texas. But neither Sheriff Marion D. Wallace nor Tom Collier, his deputy, knew what bloody drama was quickening to a climax as they rode up to the home of the five Marlow brothers, armed with a capias issued by the District Court of Wilbarger County for the arrest of Boone Marlow, on the charge of murdering James Holdson.

Sheriff Wallace dismounted at the chimney end of the cabin, where there were no doors or windows, and tied his horse. Collier swung up alongside the building and peered in the window. The brothers sat at dinner.

Boone saw the deputy's eyes fall upon him, and his thin lips tightened across his lean face. He tried not to show that he knew why the law was there.

"Light and rest your saddle, Tom," he invited huskily. "You boys eat yet?"

The deputy swung down. "But I reckon we won't eat," he said. His tall frame filled the doorway.

Sheriff Wallace stepped up behind. Together they moved into the room. Boone backed into one corner with his rifle, every muscle in his body dangerously quiet.

"We've come to get you, Boone," said the deputy. "For murder. Throw up your hands!" [1]

Boone's rifle cracked. The bullet gashed Tom Collier's temple and whipped up through the brim of his hat. A second bullet caught Wallace just above the right hip and passed through his kidneys. He fell backward out the door and collapsed on the porch. Startled, Collier sprang to shelter at the corner of the house. Boone levered a third cartridge into his rifle barrel. "I'll get that son, too!" he snarled, and headed for the door. But his brothers seized him and wrenched the gun from his grip. They notified Collier to throw away his gun and come and take care of Wallace. Collier complied. He helped them carry the sheriff inside the house, then rode for a doctor. [2]

Before the doctor arrived, Boone Marlow, heavily armed with rifle and revolvers, slapped a saddle on his horse and disappeared. Sheriff Wallace was removed to Graham, where he died just before Christmas. One of the bloodiest range feuds in Texas history had begun.

As in many of the early wars, this one also had its begin-

1. *Galveston News,* Dec. 18, 1888.
2. *Graham Leader,* Dec. 20, 1888.

ning with a dispute between large and small cattle owners.
The Marlows claimed to be small cattlemen. The other
side called them outlaws and thieves. They had been frequently charged with rustling stock, not only in Texas
but in Colorado, and disposing of it in Indian Territory,
then a haven for criminals.[3] But convictions had not been
possible, for lack of evidence in specific cases.[4]

The big cattlemen swore this was the reason rustlers
were becoming stronger and bolder. Letting men like the
Marlows operate at will was a plain invitation to others.
In an attempt to make an example of the brothers, as a
warning to the rest, James Holdson had been shot and
killed.

The wanton slaying of Sheriff Wallace, a popular
officer, was the spark which touched off the pent-up in-
dignation of all their enemies. Alf, George, Charley, and
Epp Marlow were arrested as accessories to the crime, and
every corner of the country was combed for Boone. A reward of $1,500 was offered by local citizens for his capture
and Governor Ross added $200 more if his arrest was
effected within six months. In adjoining Jack County,
Sheriff Moore and Constable Eugene Logan picked up
Boone's exhausted mount, but the killer had escaped.[5]

Failure to capture him placed his brothers in no uncertain plight. Locked in the steel cages of the Young
County jail, they soon realized that their rancher enemies

3. William MacLeod Raine, *Famous Sheriffs and Western Outlaws*, pp.
25–6.
4. *Ibid.*, p. 29.
5. *Ibid.*, p. 31.

did not intend to see them go out free men again. Collier, now acting sheriff, ordered a heavy guard kept.[6]

In the black hour before daybreak, January 17, 1889, the attack on the jail occurred. Constable Logan, Dick Cook, John Leavels, the jailer, and Deputy Sam Waggoner were taken prisoners; Leavels was forced to open the jail.

Meanwhile, Epp Marlow tore loose a water pipe and handed it to Alf, biggest and toughest of the quartet. When the masked mob jammed the door to the short, narrow passageway, they found the brothers waiting.

Alf braced his big feet wide apart, caressing the heavy pipe in his hand with almost tender care. His brothers crowded up on either side, hard-knuckled fists balled.

During all these minutes no one in either group said anything. Apparently no one wanted to. Then Charley Marlow spoke:

"The whole lot of you can't come in at once, and a few of you will never take us alive," he said grimly. "You might shoot us, but that would arouse the whole town. It's my guess you don't want the whole town to know about this."

With an angry curse one of the leaders lunged forward. Charley connected a left solidly with his chin. The man's head flopped back against the stone wall. Bleeding profusely, he slumped to the floor and lay there groaning until another member of the crowd ventured forward and carried him out.

The men in the mob were as tough as the Marlows.

6. *Ibid.*, p. 33.

They were ten to one, and the Marlows were unarmed. But they heeded the truth in Charley Marlow's words. They took stock of the grim sample of what he meant. They blustered and argued for several minutes. When they finally departed, it was with a sudden loss of appetite.[7]

But they were not through, and the Marlows knew it. A wire was sent to United States Marshal Cabell, at Dallas, informing him of the attempted lynching. Cabell immediately ordered his deputy, Ed W. Johnson, to remove the prisoners to Weatherford, Texas, for safe keeping.

Johnson was a big man, raw-boned, with square jaws and keen eyes. A year before, he had lost one hand in a shooting scrape. It had been rumored that he had been paid to protect the interests of the big cattlemen, in running down the alleged thievery in this section.[8] The Marlows believed this rumor had been circulated by his enemies until they saw the men he selected to assist him on the journey. Some of them had been in the mob that had attempted to lynch them less than two nights before!

The Marlows were taken to a blacksmith shop and shackled, two together. George and Epp made one couple, Charley and Alf the other. Then the four prisoners were placed in a hack. A man named George Martin was the driver. Marshal Johnson and the guards brought up the rear in another hack and a buggy. In the night, the cavalcade moved silently out of Graham. But there was one man who lurked in the darkness and saw them. When they

7. *Ibid.*, p. 36.
8. *Ibid.*, p. 27.

had gone, he mounted his horse and spurred away into the shadows, riding fast.

The procession crawled toward Dry Creek. Beyond, the road cut through a heavy stretch of mesquite. The teams and rigs splashed and rattled through the shallow stream, and the tenseness of the prisoners grew. As they started up the opposite bank someone in the buggy called loudly up to them. "Any you boys want a drink?"

This was the signal. Simultaneously George Martin slid out of the driver's seat, then broke and ran. Dark shadows rose from the brush to the right of the trail, and a dozen guns turned the darkness into a red hell.

Charley and Alf toppled over the side of the hack. They hit the road together, sprinting straight toward the buggy load of guards. Alf snapped a rifle from one of the men before he could use it. Charley jerked away Johnson's revolver just as the deputy's six-shooter cleared leather.

At the same time George and Epp rushed the men in the third rig. George gripped a leg and twisted one guard out on the ground. Epp clubbed him with a heavy fist and snatched his guns.

All armed now, the brothers opened fire. Shot through his one good hand, Johnson was out of the fight when it started.[9] Someone blasted quick shots from the mesquite. Alf dropped with a bullet through the brain. Epp died, riddled with rifle lead.

Leveled across the rough boards of the hack, the guns of Charley and George Marlow took their toll. Bruce

9. *Graham Leader*, Jan. 24, 1889.

Wheeler was the first bushwhacker killed. Constable Logan slithered away into the brush with a slug in his leg. Sam Cresswell died with his face in the dust.

Then a load of buckshot struck Charley in the breast. George Marlow's gun hammered out another round of lead that killed Frank Harmison, a member of the mob the night at the jail. The surviving bushwhackers and guards fled.

Charley Marlow's wound was serious. George was bleeding badly. Both were chained to their dead brothers, unable to escape with such bulks hanging to their feet. With pocket knives, they disjointed the dead men's ankles and freed themselves.

George picked up what arms and ammunition he could find, while Charley dragged himself into one of the abandoned rigs. They drove to Finis, had the chains cut from their legs, then drove to their cabin and sent for a doctor.

Dr. Price arrived. With him rode Sheriff Tom Collier and a posse. But the intrepid brothers had barricaded the house for battle. They allowed Dr. Price to enter. When he had attended their wounds, they sent him to inform Collier that they would surrender only to Marshal Cabell; that they had plenty of arms and ammunition and did not intend to be taken alive.

Collier barked orders to attack. But the posse held back. It was the opinion of the majority that enough blood had been shed by both factions. After considerable bickering among themselves, Collier agreed to the brothers' proposal. Two days later, Cabell and a deputy arrived. The two Marlows surrendered; they were removed to Dallas, placed under guard, and there recovered from their wounds.

One week later three men drove up to the sheriff's office, in a wagon, and called Tom Collier outside. In the back lay the body of Boone Marlow. He had been shot on Hell Creek, up in the Comanche Nation, resisting arrest.

Although Boone had justly paid for the murder of Sheriff Wallace, the West's code of fair play as to his brothers had been outraged. Public opinion turned at last against the ruthless tactics of the cattle combine. Law-abiding citizens came out openly and demanded that these lawbreakers also be brought to reckoning. The federal government delved into the attack at Dry Creek. Most of the survivors were indicted by a grand jury at Dallas. Some were charged with obstructing a deputy United States marshal, others with murder and conspiracy. The years dragged by. So did the cases against those indicted. Three were finally convicted, but none ever served any time. George and Charley Marlow were once again tried for rustling, but the charges against them were finally dismissed.[10]

10. William MacLeod Raine, *Famous Sheriffs and Western Outlaws,* pp. 42–4.

BUCKSHOT ON
THE BRAZOS

CHAPTER IX

Indian Justice

SILON LEWIS

A special term of the Mosholotubbe district court, of the Choctaw Nation, was in session. The setting was a white-painted council house on the western edge of Brown's Prairie, about fourteen miles southwest of the present town of Red Oak, in the wilds of the Kiamichi Mountains of southeastern Oklahoma. Indian Judge Noel J. Holsum, of the first judicial district, presided. The defendant, a fullblood Choctaw named Silon Lewis, forty years old, had just been found guilty of the slaying of Joe Hokolutubbe, another Choctaw Indian, December 10, 1892.[1]

It was a tense, solemn occasion. For a long moment following the announcement of the verdict, a heavy silence hung over the small room. Finally Judge Holsum lifted his sonorous voice:

"Silon Lewis, *minteh!*"

Tall and majestic, stoic face expressionless and his arms

1. James R. Gray, "Last Choctaw Execution," *Tulsa World*, Sept. 17, 1950.

folded across his chest, the Indian arose and approached Judge Holsum's high bench.

"Silon Lewis"—the judge repeated the defendant's name slowly—"you have been granted a fair and impartial trial by the high tribunal of our nation. It therefore becomes my duty as judge, clothed by the great power of Our Father, and I do hereby sentence you to be executed by rifle shot at twelve o'clock, high noon, on the fifth day of November, 1894. It is the command of this court that you appear at this council house at that time and on that date, prepared to pay the penalty. *Shee-ah!"*

The defendant's face showed no emotion. Arms still folded across his chest, he uttered a guttural *"O-meh,"* his acknowledgment that he understood and accepted the sentence of death. Then he turned and strode from the council house, passed quietly through the throng of spectators to his pony standing outside, mounted and rode away into the woods—unguarded and alone!

It would be nearly two years before his execution, yet he had been allowed to go free until that time. His only keeper was his conscience. Each of the Five Civilized Tribes had their own sovereign government patterned after that in Washington, with legislative, executive, and judicial branches; their statutes, courts, and trial procedure were much the same as in the white man's courts; they had Indian judges and lawyers.[2] But their criminal codes made no provision for prisons or jails. Indians had a high sense of honor. It was the teaching of their fathers. His peo-

2. Angie Debo, *And Still the Waters Run*, pp. 9–10.

ple had found Silon Lewis guilty; they must be right.[3]

Even months after his sentence was pronounced, when two white friends suggested that he flee to another territory and offered to finance the journey, Lewis replied: "White man no understand. Me same dead already."

Under the tribal laws a violator was never in custody after he was arrested and brought to the council house. The council listened to his case before a prosecutor and a representative for the defense and then passed judgment. If found guilty, the defendant was set free without further formality or delay. He was simply told to be on hand on the date fixed for punishment. There were no provisions for long-drawn appeals.

Further, the Indian laws provided only two kinds of punishment—death by the bullet and the scourging near-death of the hickory switch. The degree of punishment depended upon the crime. A hundred lashes was a good average for crimes running from larceny to manslaughter.

For a lashing, the offender was stripped to the waist. His feet were tied together and a log placed between his legs to keep them on the ground. His hands were tied and the rope thrown over a tree limb. Then the executioner went to work with a good stout switch. Sometimes a whipping post was used. In this event four men, two men to an arm, held the offender up to the post. Each time the whip came down it cut a raw, red welt across his bare back. Sometimes it was necessary to use several switches be-

3. Lon R. Stansbery, "Whip and Rifle, Indian Punishments," *Tulsa World,* July 18, 1937.
TOUGHEST OF
THEM ALL

fore the number of lashes ordered by the court had been meted out. The whippings took place on the council house lawn and were open to the public. Crowds of curious, red and white alike, came to see how the victim reacted. Some of the offenders could take it, never uttering a sound or showing any emotion. Others, however, would writhe and groan and scream with each blow and otherwise make the occasion a horrible affair.[4]

The punishment was administered by the strongest of the Lighthorse, the enforcement officers of the nation. They were mounted Indian police, selected by the council for their fearlessness and honesty. In addition, each district elected a high sheriff and under him were several deputies. The high sheriff of the Mosholotubbe district was Tecumseh Moore.

The slaying of Joe Hokolotubbe, for which Lewis had been sentenced to die, was the upshot of a disagreement in a Choctaw election. Elections in the Indian nations hardly ever were peaceful affairs. Circumstances surrounding this one went back to the years following the Choctaw migration from their old Mississippi home to the then Indian country. White "squatters" soon came pouring over the boarder from the adjoining states and territories. Many of these intruders married Indian women and took out membership in the tribe as squaw men. Soon there was a move on foot to do away with the nation's control of its land and allot it in certain amounts to each member of the tribe. The younger members favored the movement,

4. *Ibid.*

but the fullblood Choctaws bitterly opposed it. The group favoring the proposal became known as the Progressives, and Eagle was their party designation. Those opposed were called Standpatters or Nationalists, and Buzzard was the contemptuous appellation hurled at them. A bitter enmity grew between the two factions.[5]

In the race for governorship of the Choctaw tribe in 1892, Wilson N. Jones became the Progressive candidate, and Jacob Jackson ran on the Standpatter ticket. Jones was elected by such a narrow majority that a hot dispute arose.

Joe Hokolotubbe had been the leader of the Progressives, and Lewis belonged to the opposing Standpatters. Angry over the defeat of their candidate, Lewis and thirty-two Standpatters went on a rampage. They swooped down on Hokolotubbe's cabin, a mile and a half south of Hartshorne, and shot him in cold blood. News of the slaying was rushed to Green McCurtain, chief of the Choctaws. He sent a posse of Lighthorse across the mountain and placed the raiders under arrest. Lewis confessed he was the one who fired the fatal shot.[6] He was the only one of the group ever convicted of the slaying.[7]

November 5, 1894, the execution day, was a gala occasion. Indians, with their families, came from miles throughout the Mosholotubbe district. White settlers and cowboys came on horseback, in wagons, and on foot. Picnic lunches

5. Interview with Lyman Pusley, fullblood Choctaw, and last executioner under the laws of that nation.

6. *Ibid.*

7. *Eagle-Gazette*, Nov. 29, 1894.

TOUGHEST OF
THEM ALL

were spread beneath the big oak trees. Some, including the condemned man's family, camped at a small stream nearby. A force of some forty Lighthorse were on hand, Winchesters draped across their arms, to preserve order.

At fifteen minutes before noon, Lewis had not arrived. Suddenly an Indian youth came rushing into the clearing and cried that a large group of Standpatters were on their way to stop the execution. The spectators scattered for cover. The Lighthorse calmly lined up on each side of the council house, rifles ready. Some of them knelt behind a high rick of wood that had been stacked near the front door. There followed a short period of tense, nervous waiting. Every eye was glued on the surrounding oak and pine trees. Far up the mountainside a wild turkey gobbled to its mate, and down in the valley a mongrel dog set the woods echoing with a hideous, mournful howl. Then, at five minutes of twelve, Lewis appeared at the edge of the timber. He entered the clearing alone, as he had left it the day of his sentence. He was leading his pony. "Pony tired. I ride long way," he explained to High Sheriff Tecumseh Moore.[8]

He gave the pony a gentle pat and tied it to a tree. His family and friends gathered around him quickly. There is no word in the Choctaw tongue which means "goodby." There is a phrase which says, "We will be together again, somewhere, sometime," and that is what Lewis said to his family and friends. Promptly at noon he left them and walked back to Sheriff Moore.

8. Interview with Lyman Pusley.

INDIAN
JUSTICE

"Time is up. Choctaw law say must be shot. Want Lyman Pusley do it," Lewis told the sheriff.

Pusley, a deputy under Moore, was a full blood and one of Lewis' close friends.

Lewis was ordered to sit on a blanket. Two Indians stepped forward. One took Lewis' right arm, the other his left, and held them out from his sides. While in this position, the sheriff dipped his finger in a can of white powder and painted a cross on the condemned man's shirt over his heart. Then Sheriff Moore stepped back and handed Pusley his rifle.

Pusley walked back a dozen paces. He lifted the Winchester and took careful aim. For what seemed like a full minute the two friends looked steadily into each other's eyes as they bid their last farewells. Then the rifle cracked. White powder jumped from the Indian's shirt.

"The bullet went clean through the murderer's body, but missed its mark, and Lewis throwing his head back, sank groaning to the ground, blood spurting from the wound. To end the horrible work, the sheriff was finally compelled to take hold of the man's nose (after covering his face with a handkerchief) and smother him to death. He lived thirty minutes after being shot. . . ." [9]

The last legal execution under the old tribal laws of justice had been carried out. On June 7, 1897, all Indian courts were abolished by an act of Congress.[10]

9. *Eagle-Gazette,* Nov. 15, 1894.

10. U. S. Statutes at Large, 55th Congress, Session I, Vol. 30, Chapter 3, p. 83 provided that on or after January 1, 1898, the United States courts in the Indian Territory should have original and exclusive jurisdiction over all civil and criminal cases and all persons irrespective of race.

Nothing came of the threat delivered by the boy a few minutes before the execution. It proved to be only a scheme of Lewis' friends to provide as much entertainment as possible for his last day on earth.

CHAPTER X

Border Killer

ZIP WYATT

Two men faced each other at Pryor's Grove, twelve miles north of Greensburg, Kansas. They were Deputy Sheriff Andy Balfour, who wasn't afraid of any man this side of heaven or hell, and the slouching, loose-jointed youth in the black hat he had come to arrest.

The latter stood with his back to the bay horse he had just bridled. During the tense minutes which had passed since Balfour surprised him, his steady, dark eyes hadn't wavered for a second from the officer's gun hand.

The hot afternoon of July 4, 1891, made the perspiration burst from his brow and stream down his face. The air was filled with the dull roar of the celebrating crowd all around them, but the only thing the youth heard was Balfour's voice demanding his surrender.

"You stole those gloves, that riding bridle and rope," he said. "I'm taking you in."

The youth wet his dry lips. When he spoke, his soft

chilling voice carried through the grove so clearly that everyone instinctively stopped talking, as if he had suddenly yelled, "Quiet!"

What he actually said was: "Sorry, tinbadge, I can't afford to be took!"

Balfour didn't hesitate, never said another word. He moved forward to take his man in custody.

The youth's hand darted inside his shirt and out again. The first gun blast knocked the deputy off his feet. The second bullet struck him in the spine and broke his back. As he lay dying on the ground, he fired at the youth twice, hitting him in the left thigh and hand, neither wound taking serious effect. The youth leaped astride the bay, spurred through the startled crowd and disappeared in the timber with a flash of stolen accoutrements.

Thus began the crimson career of Zip Wyatt, alias Dick Yeager—the most dangerous and elusive of the early-day outlaws in Oklahoma territory.

He was born Nelson Ellsworth Wyatt, in Indiana, 1863, the second child in a family of seven boys and one girl. His father, John F. Wyatt, was a volunteer Union soldier in the eighty-fifth Indiana regiment during the Civil War. His mother was Rachel Jane Quick, whom his father met during the war and married when Rachel was sixteen. Young Wyatt grew up caring little for school or the finer influences that contribute to the development of useful manhood, frequently involving himself in brawls that gradually grew criminal. Obviously there was a bad strain somewhere in the line of family descent, for his older brother, known throughout the West as "Six-Shooter Jack," was a professional gambler and was killed over a gambling table at Texline, Texas, in 1891.[1]

When old Oklahoma was opened to settlement in 1889, the Wyatt family staked a claim on Fitzgerald Creek, ten miles northeast of Guthrie, where young Nelson met and married beautiful Miss Anna Bailey.

But neither the change of clime nor his marriage did anything to settle the youth. He was already a professional horseman and an expert shot; and, in the early days of the territory, when there was little law and less order, it became his delight to "throw his long legs over a forty-pound saddle, fill up on coffin varnish and course wildly through the settlements, whooping and yelling and firing his Colt forty-fives at fences and trees." [2]

By degrees he grew bolder, and on the night of June 3, 1891, he "got on a big jag" and shot up the little town of Mulhall in "regulation style." The citizens armed themselves, and, in the running fight which followed, two men were wounded and Zip Wyatt escaped. A warrant for his arrest was issued and placed in the hands of the Logan County sheriff, at Guthrie.

For a while, Wyatt hid out on the Cimarron, then fled to Kansas and went to work on the farm of George Cook, in the harvest. On July 4, he appeared in Greensburg and stopped for the noon hour at the livery stable of A. D.

1. *Daily Oklahoman*, Aug. 21, 1921. "The Story of the Criminal Career and Death of Dick Yeager, Oklahoma's Greatest Outlaw."

2. *Daily Oklahoma State Capital*, Aug. 9, 1895. "A Short Sketch of the Life of Dick Yeager."

III

Roberts. After he had gone, Roberts discovered he was missing a pair of riding gloves, a riding bridle, and a lariat, and called the sheriff's office. Sheriff James Bonsall being in Iowa, Deputy Balfour took the youth's trail and followed him ten miles north to Pryor's Grove, where a horse race was scheduled for that afternoon. He had attempted to arrest Wyatt in possession of the stolen equipment, and was slain.

Wyatt dashed back to the territory, where he knew the country better and had little difficulty finding safe retreats, as he shifted from one section to another, eluding posses. When Sheriff Bonsall returned from Iowa, he began a relentless search for the fugitive. A $1,000 reward was offered for Wyatt's apprehension. Fearing some of his territory cronies might double-cross him for such a large amount, Wyatt fled to Indiana. In a short time, Sheriff Bonsall learned that he was living with an aunt near his old home at Cory. At Terre Haute, he paused to enlist the aid of Sheriff Powers and four policemen. At daybreak, they surrounded a small house on the outskirts of the village and captured the killer as he sat reading at a table.[3]

Bonsall returned to Terre Haute with his prisoner. There he was detained for a week while an attempt was made to free Wyatt on a writ of habeas corpus. Finally Governor Claud Mathews ordered the fugitive surrendered to Oklahoma by prior right of first warrant, and Bonsall delivered his prisoner to the sheriff of Logan County, at Guthrie.

Bonsall did not, however, give up in his effort to have

3. *Ibid.*

the prisoner returned to Kansas for trial in the slaying of his deputy. En route to Oklahoma with Wyatt, he had stopped in Topeka and tried to persuade Governor Lyman V. Humphrey to countermand the Indiana governor's order, which Governor Humphrey refused to do, saying: "Kansas may want a prisoner returned from Oklahoma or Indiana." Thus Wyatt remained in the Guthrie jail—that is, until New Year's day, 1892.

While his case was being argued in the Guthrie territorial court, on a requisition from the governor of Kansas on the murder charge, Wyatt broke jail and again fled to his Oklahoma haunts.

He was now given the nickname of Zip because of his ability to fade in a flash when posses closed in for a capture. The situation of the country at the time also impeded the search for him. Old Oklahoma comprised only six counties and was bound on three sides by the Indian nations. To the north, the Cherokee Outlet provided perfect refuge for such gentry. For the next three years, Zip swept through the new land, spreading terror. After the Cherokee Outlet was opened for settlement, in September, 1893, Wyatt, using the alias of Dick Yeager, centered his activities in Blaine and Kingfisher counties. Officers sought him as leader of the gang who held up and robbed the Rock Island train near Dover, April 4, 1895.[4] Fred Hoffman, treasurer of "D" county, was robbed and murdered. In Blaine County, E. E. Townsend was shot down in cold blood in the robbery of his home. And, on July 26, Wyatt

4. *Stillwater Gazette,* April 11, 1895.

and a member of his gang named Isaac Black rode to the Oxley store and post office at Winview and robbed Joe Laswell of a quantity of goods and cash.[5]

A posse was organized and began scouring the country for them. Another posse headed south from the Outlet to intercept the fleeing bandits. The evening of August 1, they surrounded the outlaws in a clump of blackjack timber near Cantonment.

With guns blazing, the pair made their bid for freedom. Black was shot through the head and died instantly. Wyatt was hit in the breast and his rifle shot from his grip, but he retrieved it, shot his way through the posse and escaped on foot.

Wyatt was a man of unusual physical endurance. But his position now was uncertain. On foot, with an ugly wound sapping his energy, his only chance was to seize transportation and get out of the section immediately.

After dodging his pursuers for an hour, he came upon a boy driving a cart. He punched the lad in the ribs with his Winchester and forced him to drive at top speed to the northeast until the horse dropped from exhaustion. Cursing his luck, the killer continued on foot, eluding his pursuers again in a cane field near Enid.

Blood-stained and weary, he staggered to the home of John Daily, on Skeleton Creek, at dark, took a work horse from the farmer at gun point and rode north. A few miles farther he sighted a saddle pony in the pasture of another settler, named Will Blakely. Leaving Daily's horse behind,

5. *Daily Oklahoma State Capital,* July 30, 1895.

BORDER
KILLER

Wyatt mounted the fresh pony and headed southeast, through the night.

Meanwhile, Daily hastened to a neighbor's home, borrowed a horse and saddle, and rode to spread the alarm. At the home of Horton Miles, he found a dozen men who had just adjourned a business meeting and informed them that the killer was in the vicinity.

Two of the men joined him and hurried to the point where the outlaw had been seen last. There they waited until daylight. The others scattered, arousing the entire community. A posse composed of Sheriff Elzie Thralls and a half dozen deputies arrived from Garfield County.

Sheriff Thralls assumed command. At daybreak, the group moved southeast on Wyatt's trail. Near Sheridan, they found the stolen pony, winded and abandoned. They tracked the outlaw into a nearby cornfield.

The sheriff deployed his party. Deputy Ad Poak and a man named Tom Smith were detailed to follow in direct pursuit of the outlaw. Deputy S. T. Wood was left on guard to prevent the fugitive from seizing one of the posse's mounts and again making his escape. Other deputies and volunteers were split in pairs and posted at frequent intervals about the field. Poak and Smith then began their advance.

The trail led through the field toward a creek. They found spots in the plowed earth where the wounded outlaw had fallen and risen again, leaving stains of fresh blood. Worming their way forward, they came upon him suddenly. He was lying on the ground, rifle ready, and looking in the direction from which Thralls and his group were moving into the field. Poak and Smith leveled their guns.

"Drop that rifle, Wyatt!" Poak ordered.

Wyatt snapped to a sitting position, swinging the barrel of his Winchester in an arc, and Poak and Smith each fired in rapid succession. Their bullets struck the outlaw's body less than two inches apart, shattering his pelvic bone and entering his abdomen. Poak, still covering him with his gun, again demanded him to drop his rifle and put up his hands, and Wyatt cried, "For God's sake don't kill me," and obeyed the order.[6]

He was still alive when they carried him from the cornfield. They took him to Sheridan to a small school building where Sunday church services were just being concluded. The blackboard was removed from the wall and placed across the tops of the benches and the wounded man laid on it while he was given first aid by Doctors C. R. Jones and Frank Love.

That evening, August 4, 1895, he was taken to Enid and placed in the Garfield county jail. The jail was in the town square, surrounded by a tight, slate-colored fence with five strands of barbed wire at the top; at each corner a deputy sheriff armed with a Winchester sat on a box to prevent the elusive killer from making another escape and to keep back the crowd that came to gaze upon the celebrated desperado. Jokingly, he confessed every crime that had been committed in the territory since the opening. He kidded the lawyers who came to see him, and said, "They ain't worth the powder and salt to blow them to

6. *Ibid.*, Aug. 12, 1895.

hell." The doctors told him he would never need an attorney nor ever be tried for his crimes. He had virtually been shot to pieces. It wasn't possible that he would live.[7]

For a few days it looked as if he would prove the doctors wrong. He grew stronger and spryer. He ate from hampers of fried chicken brought in by admirers and drank cold bottles of beer. He held mock court trials from a bunk in his cell and entertained everyone who visited him. Then, one evening, his fever took a sharp rise.

"Zip," one of the doctors said, "this is the end. Is there anyone you wish to see; anything you want to confess?"

"Nobody to see, doc; nothin' to say," Wyatt replied.[8]

Throughout the sultry evening he suffered. At six minutes past midnight, on the seventh of September, he died.

The county bore the small funeral expense. Dan Bass built a cheap pine coffin the same night, while the body lay on a bench in his little carpenter shop. The next morning the body was buried in a lonely grave outside of Enid, without ceremony. The only persons present were the gravedigger, the driver of the spring wagon which had served as a hearse, and Bass, the carpenter, with his little brown dog, which had followed behind the procession.

How many crimes did the outlaw actually commit? No one really knew. Even in those last moments his dark thoughts remained his own. Like a meteor he had flashed across the border frontier and faded ingloriously.

7. Marquis James, *The Cherokee Strip*, p. 30.
8. *Ibid.*, p. 32.

CHAPTER XI

Battle on
Hell's Fringe

THE DOOLIN GANG

Although historians and other writers of pioneer tragedies and early-day events have made only sketchy reference to the "Battle of Ingalls," it was the most desperate and exciting gun-fight waged between organized banditry and peace officers of the Old West.

The battle occurred on the eastern edge of Oklahoma territory and on the western border of the lawless Indian nations, known as Hell's Fringe, the morning of September 1, 1893, fifteen days before the opening of the Cherokee Outlet. On the side of law and order was a small group of deputy United States marshals under E. D. Nix, in whose hands the federal government had placed the responsibility for wiping out the numerous outlaws that infested this newly settled section of the frontier; on the lawless side rode the notorious Bill Doolin and his gang of cutthroats and murderers.

Doolin had been a member of the famous Dalton gang that had been almost annihilated at Coffeyville, October 5, 1892, when they tried to rob two banks at once. Only Emmett Dalton survived the gun blast of irate citizens. Doolin would have been there, too, if his horse hadn't gone lame. The time it took him to obtain another mount saved his life. As he approached the outskirts of the city, a terrified rider rushed past him, shouting the news. Doolin wheeled his horse and headed back to Indian Territory, not stopping until he had reached the Dalton cave, in the Creek Nation, thirteen miles east of Ingalls and the Oklahoma territory line. Here he hid out while he laid new plans and gathered a new gang.[1]

Second in command of this new organization was Bill Dalton, brother of Grat, Emmett, and Bob, who were in the Coffeyville raid. Until then, Bill had been a respected citizen living in California and not exactly in sympathy with such activities. Now he took the vengeance trail, throwing away all pretense at respectability, and became first to join Bill Doolin.[2] Within a few weeks, about the worst lot of desperadoes the West ever produced had holed up on the Cimarron.[3] They became known as the Wild Bunch.[4]

Besides Doolin and Dalton, members of the gang at the time of the Ingalls battle were George "Bitter Creek" Newcomb, who had come from Kansas; "Red Buck"

1. Evett Dumas Nix, *Oklahombres*, pp. 45–51.
2. *Ibid.*, pp. 57–8.
3. J. A. Newsom, *Going Out of the Outlaws*, p. 169.
4. Col. H. Edwin Mootz in *The Pony Express*, Dec., 1945.

Waightman, horse thief and killer, the most surly, vicious bad man of them all; "Tulsa Jack" Blake, Dan "Dynamite Dick" Clifton, and Charlie Pierce, seasoned outlaws; and Roy Daugherty, alias Arkansas Tom Jones, who came from a family of preachers.

Within a year the gang robbed a dozen banks and trains, terrorizing the country from Southwest City, Missouri, to Ford County, Kansas, and led the marshals in one of the wildest manhunts ever conducted in Oklahoma.

Time and again, posses tried to track the outlaws to their hidden cave, but always they lost their trail in the badlands of Hell's Fringe, where the Wild Bunch seemed to vanish. Then, late in August, Marshal Nix learned that the gang was making Ingalls its headquarters.

Ingalls lay thirty-five miles northeast of Guthrie, the territorial capital. Situated far from the railroads and off the beaten trails, it seemed to have little excuse for existing, except that it enjoyed the distinction of being wild, wet, and wicked, and this was the magnet which attracted the outlaws from the territory, the Indian country, Osage Nation, and Cherokee Outlet. The only two-story building in town was a hotel run by a woman, Mary Pierce, who always kept three or four girls around and spent all her waking hours planning new diversions for her guests.[5] Down the street was the Ransom and Murray gambling hall and saloon, with its dancehall girls. The rest of the buildings consisted of three stores, a livery stable, and a dozen houses.

5. Evett Dumas Nix, *Oklahombres,* pp. 103–4.

The Pierce Hotel and the saloon became the two favorite hangouts of the Wild Bunch. Loaded with loot from their raids, they threw plenty of money around, and the girls helped separate them from their cash.[6] It was here that Bitter Creek met the Rose of Cimarron, an 18-year-old farm girl who had come with her family from Texas in the "Run of '89." She fell in love with the dashing young outlaw, and would join the gang on their nights to howl.[7] So little legitimate business was conducted that the sort of people in the community who might have informed the officers of the presence of the gang dared not do so, and only by accident did one of Nix's scouts learn that the Wild Bunch were in Ingalls celebrating the fruits of a double train robbery they had just pulled at Wharton, in the Cherokee Outlet. On August 31, Nix dispatched deputies John Hixon, Steve Burke, Tom Houston, Jim Masterson,[8] Lafe Shadley, and Dick Speed to liquidate this notorious band of criminals. Other members of the posse for the mission were George Cox, Henry Keller, Hi Thompson, and Doc Roberts.

The officers outfitted themselves with a covered wagon. Most of the posse members rode with the arms and ammunition, carefully concealed beneath the flapping canvas, so as not to attract attention. The others rode horseback. They resembled a cattle outfit on the move, a very common sight in that country since the announced opening of the Outlet.

6. Col. H. Edwin Mootz in *The Pony Express*, Dec., 1945.

7. *Ibid.*

8. Brother of the famous Bat Masterson.

The heavily armed force approached Ingalls the morning of September 1. Hixon sent Burke into town to look around. He was soon back with the report that some of the gang had just ridden in and left their horses at the livery stable. Six members—Doolin, Dalton, Red Buck, Tulsa Jack, Bitter Creek, and Dynamite Dick—had crossed the street to the saloon and started a game of poker.

Stopping the wagon in a ravine out of sight of the town, Hixon began making preparations for a siege and dispatched a message to deputies John Hale and W. M. Nix,[9] who were attending court at Stillwater, eleven miles west, to join them at once. Each member of the posse buckled two belts of cartridges about his waist, filled his pockets with additional ammunition, and armed himself with two six-shooters and a Winchester from the wagon. Then, as quietly and stealthily as possible, they began crawling into strategic positions behind buildings and trees and fences to prevent the escape of the outlaws, pending the arrival of the deputies from Stillwater.

Dick Speed drove on into town in the wagon, so as not to arouse suspicion should someone happen along and see the vehicle concealed in the ravine. He stopped the wagon in front of Light's Blacksmith Shop.

The gang was still playing poker in the saloon. They had seen Burke enter the bar, buy a drink, and ride away again, and noted that he was a stranger. Later, they had seen the covered wagon lumber into town and stop, up the street. Bitter Creek, growing nervous, left the poker game,

9. Brother of Marshal E. D. Nix.

stepped outside, carrying his rifle, and strode up the street
to the town pump. While standing there he noticed the
driver of the wagon get down and start talking to a boy
in front of a store. Bitter Creek saw the boy point in his
direction. In the next instant the man raised his rifle and
fired at Bitter Creek; thus it was he, Dick Speed, who fired
the shot that began the great fight.[10]

Speed's bullet knocked the magazine off Bitter Creek's
weapon and drove part of it into his leg. Though painfully
wounded, the outlaw jerked up his rifle and shot at Speed,
striking him in the shoulder. The weapon wouldn't work
for a second shot, because of the broken magazine.

Arkansas Tom was in a room on the upper floor of the
hotel. When he heard the first shot, he ran to the window
and saw Speed shooting at Bitter Creek. Immediately he
fired upon the officer. Speed, badly wounded, tried to
reach the door of the store. As he reached the edge of the
porch, Arkansas Tom shot the second time, killing him
instantly.[11]

This firing plunged the other officers into the fight
before they had gained their positions. There was nothing
to do but make the best of the situation. They opened
with a heavy barrage on the saloon and hotel, and the
Battle of Ingalls was on.

The youth who had pointed out Bitter Creek to Deputy
Speed, later identified as 14-year-old Jerry Simonds, was

10. Lon R. Stansbery, "Cops and Robbers, Famous Battle of Ingalls in
1893 Broke the Power of Bill Doolin's Gang," *Tulsa World*, March 21, 1937.
11. *Ibid*.

shot dead by the outlaws before he could get out of the street.[12] The atmosphere was thick with flying lead, and a citizen named N. A. Walker was wounded, and a horse that had broken loose from a hitching post was hit by a stray bullet and killed.

Bitter Creek dragged himself behind the base of the pump. Posse lead was tearing holes in the ground all around him. Jim Masterson and John Hixon had taken quick cover in a shallow ditch and were concentrating their fire on the saloon, from which most of the outlaw bullets were coming. Deputies Houston, Shadley, and Burke and the others were scattered along the street, but their positions were precarious and offered only slender protection from the deadly aim of the outlaws.

After several minutes, the firing from the saloon ceased, and it was evident that someone inside had been hit. Afterwards, it was learned that one of the saloon owners had been shot in the leg, and his partner had been wounded in the side and arm.

During the lull, Hixon sent word to Doolin that he and his gang were surrounded and that the sensible thing to do was surrender. Doolin sent back his answer:

"Go to hell!"

The battle broke loose again.

Bullets poured like hail from the hotel and from the windows and doors of the saloon, and the marshals returned the fire.

Bitter Creek still lay behind the pump, alive but helpless

12. *Ibid.*

from his wound and disabled weapon, and bleeding badly. At this stage of the fight, an amazing thing occurred.

Bitter Creek's sweetheart, Rose of Cimarron, also was in the hotel when the shooting began and had taken refuge in Bitter Creek's room on the upper floor, next to Arkansas Tom. She saw her lover's plight, and saw that he had left his six-shooters in the room, together with his belts of ammunition. The posse had every exit from the hotel covered. She could hear the bullets rip into the building. From the room occupied by Arkansas Tom, on which the fire was centered, came the crash of glass and crockery as lead shattered the dresser glass and water pitcher.

Anxious for the safety of her sweetheart, she gathered up his belts and weapons and went to a window on the sheltered side of the building. There was a chance of getting out that way; but, looking through the storm of bullets, she must have realized how utterly unsafe it was to attempt crossing the street. She must have relied upon the chivalry of the marshals. However, she had no assurance that they would not shoot down a woman. In any event, her love for this outlaw was so great that she decided to take the risk. Tossing the belts and guns outside, she climbed from the window and dropped to the ground. Flushed and breathless, she picked up the weapons. A few steps took her to the corner of the building.

Bitter Creek was a hundred feet away, and bullets were peppering the air. Holding her skirts in one hand, gripping the belts and revolvers in the other, she tore across the line of fire and reached his side.

TOUGHEST OF
THEM ALL

Startled by the sudden appearance of the girl, the marshals stopped shooting, and held their fire even as Bitter Creek opened on them with both guns, until she had reached the safety of the stable.

Doolin quickly took advantage of the situation. He darted from the saloon, ran to Bitter Creek, and, holding the wounded outlaw up with one hand, half carried, half dragged him to the livery barn.

As they reached the door, a bullet from the posse struck Doolin in the foot. He and Bitter Creek both fell but managed to crawl into the stable.

At the same instant, Red Buck, Tulsa Jack, Dynamite Dick, and Bill Dalton, with guns blazing, rushed from the saloon and also headed for the stable and their horses.

This series of surprising, daring moves threw the officers into confusion. Situated on the side of the street to which the outlaws ran, it was necessary to shift positions to shoot effectively, which they were unable to do in the face of the quartet's sudden, fierce onslaught, and the four reached their destination without being hit.

So far as escape was concerned, the outlaws now had the advantage. The marshals commenced a steady stream of fire at the stable entrance and windows.

Deputy Houston ran for a point where he could cover the rear exit. Arkansas Tom's window commanded the street, but the fire was so heavy upon his room he was unable to help his comrades when they dodged from the saloon to reach the stable door. Dragging his rifle, he had crawled up a ladder into the hotel attic and, with the muz-

zle of the weapon, poked a hole through the shingle roof.
He thrust the barrel through and shot from there, killing
Deputy Houston before the latter gained a dozen yards.[13]

The outlaws opened a barrage from the stable. Lafe
Shadley ran from cover and dropped behind the carcass of
the dead horse in the street. From this point, he poured a
hot leaden reply that drove the outlaws back from the
door.

Inside the barn, Bitter Creek, weak and bleeding, was
helped astride his horse. The Rose mounted in front of
him and he clung around her waist with both arms. Red
Buck, Tulsa Jack, and Dynamite Dick mounted their
horses. Then Doolin, hobbling on his wounded foot, and
Dalton stepped back to the front of the stable and poured
a withering fire into the street from the windows on each
side of the door, holding the marshals at bay while the
rest of the gang rode from the rear of the building into a
draw. Finally, both Doolin and Dalton, firing a last volley,
also mounted and rode from the barn.

At the head of the draw, Bitter Creek, too weak from
loss of blood, had lost his grip around Rose and fallen to
the ground. The Rose had dismounted to help him back
into the saddle. Shadley had run from the shelter of the
dead horse to the corner of the stable and was taking aim
at Bitter Creek when Dalton and Doolin both poured four
shots into his body, killing him.[14] The outlaws were in the

13. The Territory of Oklahoma vs. Tom Jones, Case No. 323, District
Court, Payne County, Oklahoma Territory.

14. *Stillwater Gazette*, Sept. 1, 1893.

clear now and they galloped from the town into the safety of the badlands along the Cimarron.

They seemed to have forgotten their comrade in the hotel attic, who continued shooting. Quickly the posse surrounded the building and kept firing into the roof and upstairs until it was virtually riddled with bullets. It was a miracle how Arkansas Tom remained alive, but after two hours, he was still taking pot shots at the officers and seemed to have an inexhaustible supply of ammunition.

It was impossible for the marshals to enter the building and capture him. There was no inside stairway. An outside ladder was the only means of reaching the second floor, and the concealed outlaw was able to cover the ladder entrance.

By this time Deputies John Hale and W. M. Nix arrived, with a posse from Stillwater. A group of eleven men went in pursuit of the outlaws who had escaped, and the others held a conference while keeping the hotel covered. Jim Masterson offered the best solution of the problem and volunteered to carry it out. While the others kept the outlaw busy on the ladder side of the hotel, Masterson gathered some dry brush and hay and crept to the opposite side of the structure. Mrs. Pierce, noticing what was going on, called out to the officers to spare her place. She said it contained everything she owned and was her only means of livelihood, and if they would not set it on fire, she would make Arkansas Tom surrender.

The officers agreed to wait to see what she could do.

The frightened woman went to the foot of the ladder and called to the outlaw, then climbed up and went inside. Within a short time she came to the window and told them if Arkansas Tom was promised protection from mob violence and not to be placed in chains, he would give himself up. She said that he knew he could be taken finally, but in the meantime he would kill at least seven men whom he had range on at that moment, and he had over eighty rounds of ammunition left. His proposition was accepted, and Arkansas Tom, bleeding from his bullet wounds, came down the ladder and surrendered to the marshals.

The outlaws who had escaped from the fight found comparative safety at the cave, and the posse scoured the country for days without being able to discover their river hideout. Meanwhile, the beautiful Rose carried the outlaws medicine and bandages to take care of their wounds, and kept them informed as to the movements of the officers.

Two outlaws wounded and only one prisoner taken was not a fair exchange for the lives of an innocent boy and three United States men. But the Battle of Ingalls was the beginning of the end of the Doolin gang.

Arkansas Tom was indicted and tried in the territorial court at Stillwater, before Judge Frank Dale, for the slaying of Deputy Marshal Tom Houston, and sentenced to fifty years in prison at Lansing.[15] He was paroled in 1910, his parole revoked in 1917, when he went back to prison for

15. The Territory of Oklahoma vs. Tom Jones, Case #323, District Court, Payne County, Oklahoma Territory.

a bank robbery in Missouri,[16] and, in 1924, shortly after his release, he was shot and killed by the police while robbing another bank at Joplin.[17]

The Rose of Cimarron was taken into custody for aiding the outlaws. She was convicted in federal court at Guthrie and sentenced to four years in the reformatory at Farmington, Massachusetts. After her release, she turned respectable and married a prominent citizen of Oklahoma. Those who knew her true identity swore never to reveal it, and they never did.

Bill Dalton was the first of the Doolin gang to meet death. He was tracked down by the marshals and slain by Deputy Loss Hart, as he fled from a ranch house near Ardmore, in the Chickasaw Nation.

Tulsa Jack was killed May 5, 1895, following the holdup of the Rock Island train at Dover. Red Buck, who also had participated in the robbery, escaped. He was located hiding in a dugout near Arapaho, and slain by Deputy Chris Madsen and his posse.

Bitter Creek and Charlie Pierce were killed after they sought refuge at the Dunn brothers' ranch, near Pawnee.

Dynamite Dick was shot by Deputies Burke, Nix, and Jones following a gun battle near Blackwell.

Bill Doolin had developed rheumatism from the wound in his foot. He went to Eureka Spring, Arkansas, and was

16. Transcript of criminal record of Tom Jones, alias Roy Daugherty, and letter received from Kansas State Penitentiary, Nov. 1, 1951.

17. Transcript of criminal record of Tom Jones, alias Roy Daugherty, and letter received from Missouri State Penitentiary, November 6, 1951.

captured in a bath house there by Deputy Bill Tilghman. He was returned to Guthrie and lodged in jail, but, on the night of July 5, 1896, he escaped.

Deputy Marshal Heck Thomas took his trail and followed him to the home of his wife's parents, at Lawson. Doolin came up the trail at midnight. Thomas called to him to throw up his hands and surrender. Instead, Doolin raised his Winchester. Thomas fired his shotgun once and the outlaw leader fell dead, riddled with twenty-one buckshot.

Thus ended the careers of the Wild Bunch. A few years later, the town of Ingalls moved, and only the old Ransom and Murray saloon and Pierce Hotel were left standing in its memory. For a long time afterwards, a curious investigator could pause inside their decaying walls, dig lead from the rotten wood, and try to visualize what had happened. Today, nothing is there. Only weeds stand waist high in the street where the bitter battle was fought between United States marshals and Oklahoma's most desperate gang of criminals, fifty-eight years ago.

CHAPTER XII

Toughest of Them All

CHEROKEE BILL

Take the records of John Wesley Hardin, Bill Longley, Black Jack Ketchum, Sam Bass, or any of the other Western desperadoes, and they can be considered "small potatoes" when compared with Cherokee Bill, the most noted renegade to infest the Oklahoma country in the '90s when "there was no Sunday west of St. Louis, no God west of Fort Smith."

Only eighteen years of age when his career of crime was brought to a close by Judge Isaac C. Parker, the "hanging judge" at Fort Smith, Arkansas, he was credited with being the most fiendish murderer of all those appearing in the annals of this famous court.

For more than three years he terrorized this wild country, then known as Indian Territory, and no one cared to attempt to capture him, and at least one town, in the interest of preserving the lives of its citizens, passed an ordinance making it a misdemeanor for anyone to molest him when he was abroad within its limits.[1] Not until a reward of $1,300 was offered for him, dead or alive, did the federal officers begin making plans for his capture.

He was born Crawford Goldsby at Fort Concho, Texas, February 8, 1876. When he was seven, his parents moved to Indian Territory, settling near Fort Gibson. He was a mixture of races. His mother was half negro, one-fourth Cherokee and one-fourth white. His father was of Mexican extraction, mixed with white and Sioux.[2]

"Stand up for your rights; don't let anybody impose on you," they counseled him.

At the age of fourteen he killed his brother-in-law in an argument over some hogs, and "in fiendish glee filled his body full of bullet holes."[3] After that, he flashed across the criminal annals of the territory, killing principally for the love of shedding blood. The briefness of his tumultuous career shows that he was more dangerous than intelligent.

In one respect he was a good deal like the modern bandit. He was "a hand with women." He had a sweetheart in nearly every section of the country which he traveled, but the one he loved best was Maggie Glass, the cousin of Ike Rogers, a Cherokee Indian, formerly a deputy United States marshal, and intimately acquainted with the killer.

1. *Indian Journal,* Feb. 1, 1895. "The citizens of Lenapah, I. T., have evidently been thoroughly cowed by Cherokee Bill, the outlaw; they have passed an ordinance which grants him the privilege of coming and going when he desires and they guarantee him protection from molestation."

2. S. W. Harman, *Hell on the Border,* p. 387.

3. *Ibid.,* p. 386.

United States Marshal George J. Crump, of Fort Smith, conceived the idea of having Cherokee Bill meet the girl at Rogers' home near Lenapah; and, on the night of January 29, 1895, on Rogers' invitation, the couple met. The girl suspected treachery and warned Bill to leave.

The bandit laughed viciously. "Let Rogers make his play," he snapped. "I'll show him just how long it takes to commit murder."

But Rogers was foxy. He knew the type of criminal he was dealing with. For thirty-six hours he watched and waited for a chance to get the drop on the boy bandit, while the latter visited with Maggie. Finally, about four o'clock in the morning, as Rogers leaned from his chair punching the fire with a heavy poker, Bill turned to glance at Clint Scales, a neighbor and ally of Rogers, who appeared in the doorway. In the same instant, Rogers swung the poker. It struck the killer a solid blow across the back of the head, knocking him to his knees. Then both men jumped upon Bill and bound him with baling wire, while Rogers' wife disarmed him. He was placed in chains and handcuffed and delivered to Deputy Marshals Bill Smith and George Lawson, who, in accordance with prearrangements, were waiting at Nowata.[4]

Among the first of scores of crimes Bill was charged with having committed was the robbery and slaying of a railroad agent named Richards, in Nowata. He had ridden with the notorious Bill Cook gang of outlaws when they were surprised by a posse of Indian police at Fourteen Mile

4. *Indian Chieftain*, Feb. 7, 1895.

Creek, in the Cherokee Nation. In this battle, Lighthorse-
man Sequoyah Houston was slain. He rode with the Cook
gang in the robbery of Scales' store, at Wetumka, Creek
Nation; the robbery of Parkinson's store, at Okmulgee; the
express office holdup, at Choteau; the train robbery, at Co-
retta; the hijacking of A. E. Donaldson, in the Cherokee
Nation; and the robbery of Schufelt & Son's store and post
office, at Lenapah, when he deliberately shot down an unarmed citizen, Ernest Melton.[5] Many more crimes of vary-
ing degree were charged to him, but investigation was use-
less in the face of indictment for these more serious charges.
At Fort Smith, he promptly went on trial and was convicted for the slaying of Melton,[6] and Judge Parker sentenced him to die on the scaffold.[7]

This was during the latter years of Judge Parker's tenure
on the bench, after Congress had passed an act providing
that the right of appeal from the Fort Smith court would
be allowed in all cases of conviction where the punishment
provided was death. Cherokee Bill appealed his conviction,
and Judge Parker issued a stay of execution.[8] While in jail
awaiting the Supreme Court's decision, he became impa-
tient and unruly.

There were fifty-nine men in "murderers' row" at the
time. All were given the freedom of the floor and allowed
to mingle with the other prisoners during the day, but at
night they were locked in separate cells. A more desper-

5. S. W. Harman, *Hell on the Border*, pp. 386, 392–3.
6. *Cherokee Advocate*, March 6, 1895.
7. *Indian Chieftain*, April 18, 1895.
8. *Ibid.*, May 9, 1895.

ate crew never existed, and Bill was the worst of the lot.

Someone smuggled him a six-shooter. To wind up his career with a grand finale, he shot and killed Guard Lawrence Keating, on the evening of July 26, as the latter came to lock him in his cell, then attempted the wholesale delivery of more than 250 prisoners held in the federal jail.

Other guards came running at the sound of the shot that killed Keating. They began a sniping match with Bill. Every time he fired he gobbled. It was a crazy, wild sound, half like the howl of a coyote and half like the gobble of a turkey cock. It was the death cry among the territory Indians. More than a hundred shots were fired from Winchesters and revolvers before the killer ceased gobbling and surrendered his weapon.[9]

He was tried again, this time for the murder of Keating, and Judge Parker sentenced him the second time to be hanged.[10] In pronouncing his sentence, the austere, white-haired Parker, who ordered 160 men to die and hanged 80 of them, delivered the most hair-raising denouncement ever heard in the Fort Smith halls of justice. He said:

"You are undoubtedly the most ferocious monster, and your record more atrocious than all the criminals who have hitherto stood before this bar. To effect your capture brave men risked their lives and it was only by the keenest strategy that it was effected. Even after you had been placed within the prison walls your ferocity prevented docility, and your only thought was to break away that you might

9. *Oklahoma City Times-Journal,* Aug. 2, 1895.
10. *Indian Chieftain,* Aug. 15, 1895.

return to the scenes of bloodshed from which an outraged law had estranged you. In order to make your escape you would have trampled under foot the will of the people, and releasing hundreds of your ilk, fled to your mountain and forest haunts, there to gather around you a larger and more blood-thirsty band; there to defy all power under heaven while you indulged your passion for crime; there to burn and pillage and destroy the lives of whoever stood for a moment in the way of your campaign of destruction. . . .

"It is too bad that courts can go no further than destroy life and that one execution must serve to mete justice to the multiplex murderer, the same as to those who have only one such crime for which to answer. . . ."

At 2:00 P.M., March 17, 1896, Crawford Goldsby, alias Cherokee Bill, accompanied by George Maledon, the Prince of Hangmen, made his death walk to the gallows in the jail yard jammed with six-hundred spectators. As he stood on the trap with Maledon strapping his ankles together, Marshal Crump read the death warrant. When the marshal had finished, he asked:

"Do you want to say anything to the crowd?"

"No," replied Cherokee Bill. "I came here to die—not to make a speech."

The bolt was released, and the killer fell through the trap to his death.

BIBLIOGRAPHY

Books

Barnard, Evan G., *A Rider of the Cherokee Strip*. Houghton Mifflin Company, The Riverside Press, Cambridge, 1936.

Beal, Merrill D., *The Story of Man in Yellowstone*. The Caxton Printers, Ltd., Caldwell, Idaho, 1949.

Birney, Hoffman, *Vigilantes: A Chronicle of the Rise and Fall of the Plummer Gang of Outlaws in and About Virginia City in the Early '60's*. Penn Publishing Company, Philadelphia, 1929.

Burch, J. P., *Charles W. Quantrill: A True History of His Guerrilla Warfare on the Missouri and Kansas Border During the Civil War of 1861 to 1865*. Vega, Texas, 1923.

Burns, Walter Noble, *The Saga of Billy the Kid*. Doubleday, Page and Company, New York, 1926.

Canton, Frank M., *Frontier Trails*. Houghton Mifflin Company, New York, 1930.

Coe, George, *Frontier Fighter*. Houghton Mifflin Company, New York, 1934. (University of New Mexico Press, Albuquerque, 1951.)

Dale, Edward Everett, *Cow Country*. The University of Oklahoma Press, Norman, 1945.

———, *The Range Cattle Industry*. The University of Oklahoma Press, Norman, 1930.

Debo, Angie, *And Still the Waters Run*. Princeton University Press, Princeton, New Jersey, 1940.

Dick, Everett, *The Story of the Frontier*. Tudor Publishing Company, New York, 1941.

Driggs, Howard R., *Westward America*. J. B. Lippincott Co., New York, 1942.

Eaton, Frank, *Pistol Pete: Veteran of the Old West*. Little, Brown and Company, Boston, 1952.

Gard, Wayne, *Frontier Justice*. University of Oklahoma Press, Norman, 1949.

Gardiner, Dorothy, *West of the River*. Thomas Y. Crowell Company, New York, 1941.

Hafen, LeRoy R., and Rister, Carl Coke, *Western America: the Exploration, Settlement and Development of the Region Beyond the Mississippi*. Prentice-Hall, Inc., New York, 1941.

Haley, J. Evetts, *Charles Goodnight, Cowman and Plainsman*. University of Oklahoma Press, Norman, 1949.

Harman, S. W., *Hell on the Border*. Phoenix Publishing Co., Fort Smith, Arkansas, 1898.

Hendricks, George D., *The Bad Man of the West*. The Naylor Company, San Antonio, 1942.

Hough, Emerson, *The Story of the Outlaw*. Grosset and Dunlap, New York, 1907.

James, Marquis, *The Cherokee Strip, A Tale of an Oklahoma Boyhood*. The Viking Press, New York, 1946.

———, *The Raven: A Biography of Sam Houston*. The Bobbs-Merrill Company, Indianapolis, 1929.

Lake, Stuart N., *Wyatt Earp, Frontier Marshal*. Houghton Mifflin Company, Boston, 1931.

Langford, Nathaniel Pitt, *Vigilante Days and Ways*. A. C. McClurg and Company, Chicago, 1912.

McCarty, John L., *Maverick Town, the Story of Old Tascosa*. University of Oklahoma Press, Norman, 1946.

McCoy, Joseph G., *Historic Sketches of the Cattle Trade of the West and Southwest*. Ramsey, Millett and Hudson, Kansas City, 1874.

Newsom, J. A., *Life and Practice of the Wild and Modern Indian: the Early Days of Oklahoma*. (Going Out of the Outlaws, Chapters VI–IX.) The Harlow Publishing Co., Oklahoma City, 1923.

Nix, Evett Dumas, *Oklahombres*. Eden Publishing House, St. Louis and Chicago, 1929.

Otero, Miguel Antonio, *The Real Billy the Kid*. Rufus Rockwell Wilson, New York, 1936.

Paxson, Frederic L., *Last American Frontier*. The Macmillan Company, New York, 1922.

Raine, William MacLeod, *Famous Sheriffs and Western Outlaws*. Doubleday, Doran and Company, Garden City, New York, 1929.

Richardson, Albert D., *Beyond the Mississippi*. American Publishing Company, Hartford, Conn., 1867.

Ridings, Sam P., *The Chisholm Trail*. Co-operative Publishing Company, Guthrie, Oklahoma, 1936.

Siringo, Charles A., *A Texas Cowboy, or, Fifteen Years on the Hurricane Deck of a Spanish Pony*. M. Umbdenstock and Company, Publishers, Chicago, 1885.

———, *Riata and Spurs*. Houghton Mifflin Company, New York, 1927.

Sutton, Fred E., *Hands Up!* The Bobbs-Merrill Company, Indianapolis, 1927.

Thoburn, Joseph B., and Wright, Muriel H., *Oklahoma, A History of the State and Its People*. (4 Vols.) Lewis Historical Publishing Company, Inc., New York, 1929.

Webb, Walter Prescott, *The Great Plains*. Ginn and Company, New York, 1931.

Wellman, Paul I., *The Trampling Herd, the Story of the Cattle Range in America*. Carrick and Evans, New York, 1939.

White, Owen P., *Lead and Likker*. Minton, Balch and Company, New York, 1932.

Wright, Robert M., *Dodge City, the Cowboy Capital*. Wichita Eagle Press, Wichita, Kansas, 1913.

WPA Writers Project, Compiled by, *Kansas, A Guide to the Sunflower State*.

Newspapers

Amarillo News and Globe. (Golden Anniversary Edition) 1938.

Beaver Herald. Feb.–Dec., 1895; Jan.–Dec., 1898.

Cherokee Advocate. March, 1895.

Daily Oklahoman. Jan.–June, 1896; Jan.–March, 1904; Feb., 1915; March, 1930; July–Sept., 1905; Aug.–Dec., 1895; Jan.–June, 1896; Aug., 1921; July, 1936.

Daily Oklahoma State Capital. April, 1895; July–Aug., 1895; Dec., 1896.

Eagle Gazette. Nov., 1894.

Edmond Sun-Democrat. July–Aug., 1895.

El Reno News. May–Dec., 1896.

Galveston News. Dec., 1888.

Graham Leader. Dec., 1888; Jan., 1889.

Guthrie Daily Leader. Aug., 1894; Jan., 1895; April, 1939.

Houston Post. (Centennial Edition) 1936.

Indian Chieftain. Feb.–Aug., 1895.

Indian Journal. Feb., 1895.

Kansas City Star. (Various dates.)

Oklahoma City Times-Journal. Feb.–Oct., 1895; Aug., 1895; Dec., 1907.

South and West. May–Oct., 1896.

Stillwater Gazette. Sept., 1893; April, 1895.

Thayer Headlight. April, 1873.

Vinita Leader. May, 1896.

Woodward News. April, 1900; 1905–6.

Periodicals

Collections of the Kansas State Historical Society, 1926–1928. Vol. XVII.

Montana Historical Society Collections, Vol. II.

TOUGHEST OF
THEM ALL

Pamphlets and Magazines

Hendron, J. W., *The Story of Billy the Kid: New Mexico's Number One Desperado*. Rydal Press, Inc., Santa Fe, New Mexico, 1948.

Mootz, Colonel H. Edwin, "Rose of Cimarron," *The Pony Express,* Placerville, California, Dec., 1945.

Articles

"Cops and Robbers, Famous Battle of Ingalls in 1893 Broke the Power of Bill Doolin's Gang." *Tulsa World,* March 21, 1937.

"Last Choctaw Execution." *Tulsa World,* Sept. 17, 1950.

"Life of Frank Eaton." *Guthrie Daily Leader,* April 16, 1939.

"Pistol Pete, A Biography of Frank Eaton." *Tulsa World,* May 19, 1935.

"Whip and Rifle, Indian Punishments." *Tulsa World,* July 18, 1937.

Miscellaneous

Records of the Kansas State Penitentiary, Lansing, Kansas.

Records of the Missouri State Penitentiary, Jefferson City, Missouri.

Territory of Oklahoma vs. Tom Jones, Case Number 323, District Court, Payne County, Oklahoma Territory, May 17–21, 1894.

INDEX